Remembrances
AND OTHER OBSERVATIONS

don david Calderon y Aroesty
Graphic Illustrations by Alex Close

PAGE PUBLISHING
Conneaut Lake, PA

First originally published by Page Publishing 2022

ISBN 978-1-6624-5132-4 (pbk)
ISBN 978-1-6624-5133-1 (digital)

Printed in the United States of America

Contents

Remembrances: An Introduction

This is a book with more than fifty short stories

Factual, truthful, nonfiction short stories

The short stories are about human behavior
In challenging circumstances; taken together
This is history; it is geography, it is philosophy
Perhaps some theology; all part of a crime drama

About a very difficult horrific time for the universe
An especially difficult horrific time for Europe, And
For the Jewish people caught in Nazi Europe;
It was the era of the Holocaust

But, this is a book of stories focused on the heroes,
Heroines and some exceptional gratifying events

An effort has been made to collect these stories
And to rewrite them as prose poetry vignettes
To help us all of every faith and nationality
To keep the light burning for all of the victims
By remembering some heartening events

This is intended to be a lesson plan which raises
Respect for the millions who died and those
Who barely survived. By paying careful attention
To the details of those exceptional instances

I am not a survivor of the Holocaust myself

I am not a direct descendant of either survivors or
Victims who perished in that tragedy

Why was I motivated to assemble the remembrances?
Let me try to shed some light on that question first.

The remembrances begin on page 21.

Lessons

Visiting, learning, remembering; reliving the lessons of yesteryear
Holding our collective breath that it will never be necessary again
Never be necessary again, to mobilize millions of men
To meet and defeat monsters, dripping blood from their teeth
(From the afterwords of "Leaves Quietly Applauding" about Normandy)

This book has been assembled for our children,
Grandchildren and other generations yet to be born
Of every faith and nationality, may they know
That the lessons of the Holocaust are many
And they are universal, not limited to any one time

As with any other subject of substance
What is required of you is curiosity first
Then. thoughtful appraisal and analysis
Followed by a commitment, a call to action
What will you do? What will you do to
Help make your community, nation, world
A better place to be, a better place for all

Hate is noisy, love, care, consideration mostly quiet
When reading these remembrances, try to imagine
Imagine yourself in the role of hero or heroine
You will understand at once, that heroes do not need
To fly without wings, or wear a special uniform
To perform minor miracles for the common good

Marion Pritchard saved new born babies by her "missions of disgrace"
Aristides de Sousa Mendes led a caravan of stateless refugees out of Vichy
Aryan wives refused to give up loving their Jewish husbands
Giorgio Perlasca, an Italian, spoke Spanish diplomatically in Hungary
Mauricio Hochschild (not literally) spit in a Bolivian dictator's soup
Henryk Goldszmit invented Mr. Rogers before he appeared on TV
The whole of the Denmark people rose up like a whale in the ocean to national greatness
Agnes Klein Keleti did a triple double jump from the trapeze of death
Irena Sendler, an ordinary Polish woman, decided every day that right was right, and
worthy of risking her life for the lives of children, strangers to her
Dr. Adelaide Hautval did not know that defending human dignity was a capital crime

Pino Lella skied like a dancing shepherd to lead his sheep to peace and safety
Marthe Cohn won the German order of merit for serving as a nurse, while spying on them
Amazing Grace, the white mouse, did soberly outdrink and outthink her Nazi foes
Dr. Chaim Bernard wrote a letter to the international *New York Times*

Why This Author?

1. I AM EIGHTY-ONE YEARS OLD. I was an infant during World War II and the Holocaust. I have no special insight or entitlement to tackle this project. I did so reflexively when other life experiences caused me to believe the details about the Holocaust were disappearing. Understanding that six million Jews were murdered is, of course, indelibly the essence of the Holocaust, but it is not the whole of the story.

2. I DIED (FROM AN INCIDENT OF CARDIAC ARREST) ON SEPTEMBER 21, 2012. I was miraculously and fortuitously revived by strangers (two secret servicemen and an entire crew of New York City Fire Department EMTs); all on the scene prior to any call. I am being permitted to live an extended full, long, healthy life, thanks to the actions of strangers imposing obligations on the beneficiary. I take and took those obligations seriously. See "Fortuitous Circumstances" and "Second Chance" in the appendix.

3. I AM SEPHARDIC (JEWISH FROM SPAIN PRIOR TO 1492). During the 1940s, there remained a large population of Sephardic people in Turkey (where they were protected) and in Greece and the Balkans (where they were demolished almost entirely). My extended family had lived in Macedonia for over four hundred years. Almost all of the Jews of Macedonia were killed by the Nazis in March of 1943. When I first saw "the list," it had a lasting impact on me. See "The List" and "March of 1943" in the appendix

4. I WAS EXTRAORDINARILY FORTUNATE TO PARTICIPATE AND PLAY A PART IN THE EVENTS OF 1991–1992, WHICH CULMINATED IN THE REVOCATION OF THE 1492 EDICT OF EXPULSION BY KING JUAN CARLOS OF SPAIN ON MARCH 31, 1992. This experience, which took up a significant part of two years of my life, was both a history lesson and a course on tolerance and intolerance, during which I had the benefit of being the personal pupil of Haham Rabbi Solomon Gaon, former chief Sephardic rabbi in the United Kingdom and a professor at Yeshiva University in New York and also of the Spanish people we encountered. "A Brush with History" in the appendix and "Tolerance and Intolerance."

5. FRIENDS HELPED ME UNDERSTAND. Two friends, in particular, Boris Kottler ("He Hid in the Woods") and Fred Knobloch ("Voices and Echoes"). Boris spoke about the Holocaust and his experiences at our local synagogue. He was eloquent and understanding; nervous to be a public speaker but forthright and clear about what happened to him. More than twenty years ago, I wrote my first words about the Holocaust inspired by Boris. Fred almost exactly shared our birth date in April 1940, but I was born in the safety of Brooklyn, New York, in the USA while he was born in Krakow, Poland, one of the riskiest places on earth in that era. He too has been mostly quiet and understated about his life experiences, but standing shoulder to shoulder with Fred has been a maturing experience. Boris's and Fred's lives are lessons that,

but for the grace of God and actions of some good people, we are all vulnerable. There are no exemptions when ill winds turn into tornadoes.

6. NO ONE ALIVE TODAY, AT THE BEGINNING OF THE TWENTY-FIRST CENTURY, CAN AVOID SEEING MANY ELEMENTS OF RACIAL AND RELIGIOUS ENMITY ALL OVER THE GLOBE. In my view of it, one does not need to have been a direct victim of the Holocaust or a descendant of someone who suffered thusly to be qualified to speak up now. See "Qualifications." We all have a duty to one another to act unselfishly for causes of right and decency and mutual respect. By focusing my lens on some heroes and heroines of every description, it is my intention both to honor the millions who perished in the Holocaust and those who survived while providing a lesson plan in life for all of us willing to play a constructive role in the future.

7. I expect that there may be constructive criticism of my choice of poetry or prose poetry to communicate these short stories. See "Prose Poetry." To those who ask why I selected this medium, let me answer frankly. I did not choose it; it chose me. Many of the short stories came into my head on first reading the facts I was proposing to write about. About 90 percent of the short stories are about people and events that are in the public domain and not private information. You can check the facts yourself on Google or otherwise. You will find and should find the same facts as set forth in these presentations. I wanted to express these remembrances in a way most likely to assure and ensure the details and the importance of remembering. From "Saplings from a Chestnut Tree" about Anne Frank:

    The Holocaust deniers deny
    The Holocaust deniers deny the concentration camps
    The Holocaust deniers deny the camps were used
    As mechanized killing machines to eliminate the innocent

    The Holocaust deniers deny
    That Annaliese Marie Frank ever existed

    Or from "The Greatest Gymnast Ever" about Agnes Klein Keleti:

    They didn't give any prizes for dealing with the Holocaust
    If they did, she would surely win,
    She did a triple double jump from the trapeze of death
    To the invisible, only barely imaginable
    Floor, bars and balance beams of real life

There are multiple other examples. I have poetic pride in my expression of those thoughts and my choices of words and phrases. That pride is justified if the choices have been properly utilized to elevate the facts. I often add to the stories with "afterwords" distinguished by boldface and sometimes a more personal opinion view of the matters being discussed

8. These are fifty-five short stories out of many hundreds that might have been written. They are divided into three volumes. There is no critical reason for the division. The poems in volume 1 were selected and organized as representative of my writing about two years before in

9

connection with a creative writing class assignment and submission to a poetry contest. The poems in volume 3 were selected and organized by me as a way in which I wanted to complete this book. The poems in volume 2 were then selected and organized by me in deciding which additional ones I had written to be included in *Remembrances*. There are times that two or three of them may seem to fit together. More often, the order is random. The Holocaust was ongoing and going on in all the disparate parts of Europe simultaneously. I do not suggest that the stories I have chosen to tell are in any way preferred or preferable to other stories, many of which have been written based on the personal experiences of the authors or persons close to them. I urge others with published stories to promote the reading of their stories, and I most surely wish others with unpublished stories of their own or a family member to make sure that it too is publicly known.

Qualifications

How dare me, dare to write about the Holocaust
Who am I? Who am I to publicly propound
I am not a Holocaust survivor or family member
I am not a direct descendant of anyone involved

I am, we are all, brother and sister to them
The children, grandchildren, great grandchildren
Of the ashes which first appeared, then disappeared
In the smoke smoldering over an entire continent

I am, we all are, indirect descendants of the living
Survivors of the Holocaust, who brought their memories back with them
Carried the recollections, invisible marks in their brains
On their faces, within each hug, kiss, laugh, and conversation

Transmitted magically to the next generation of us
Sometimes without words, pictures or any code at all
I am, we are, walking in the shoes left on the shore in Budapest
Without ever being in Budapest, I have never been in Budapest

I have never been in Auschwitz or in Treblinka
I have never been required to wear a prison uniform
With a yellow badge of honor, intending dishonor
I have never witnessed the sudden death of large groups of innocents

Or innocence, a society, any society, nation or people
Being trampled, crushed, tanks advancing without opposition
Soldiers firing machine guns at everyone, no one specifically, women and children
Always among the dead and dying; airplanes flying nowhere, up in the air, releasing
from their bomb bays, miscellaneous messages of hate amplifying these tragic tragedies

How dare me, us, not try to write, record our thoughts, about the Holocaust
So, I did not personally experience it: So, I was not on that continent then
We, all of us 20th-Century humans, personally experience it, indirectly
You did not need to be there, to be there; you are here, it sleeps within your skin
It's in your brain, the memory bank, and slowly surely seeps into our blood
We are required to remember, never to forget; Always to spend the time
To spend a fraction of the time to study, to learn, to recollect, to stand up
to what transpired, to be correct, history is our guide, hope is the last to die.

don david Calderon y. Aroesty
December 6, 2020

Prose Poetry

Prose poetry is to poetry what
Convertibles are to automobiles
They are both designed to get you there
From the starting point to the destination

But, prose poetry pieces, like convertible cars
Promise and provide open-air scenic views
Breezes along the way, unrestrained and unrestricted
driving, the stanzas not exactly fixed in number or in lines

There is no definite requirement of form and rhymes
As long as it is readable, readily comprehended, easily
And much more importantly, the poem is memorable, remember-able
With at least some words and phrases which stick in the reader's mind

As is the case with any vehicular traffic communication, sharp left turns
From the right lane may not be made with prose poetry, either
The author is instructed to stick to the subject, the object, the point of it
Prose poems in those cases permit your thoughts to flourish, grow brilliantly

They are flowers in the wind speeding but not so hastily as to lose their leaves
The authorities have given you literary permission, a bright green light
So to speak, for a most liberal interpretation of poetry's rules, in order to create
An allowance for you to say what you mean, but only if you mean what you say.

don david Calderon y. Aroesty
November 19, 2020

Genya's Story

(A dear friend, a lovely lady born Genya told this to me)

On September first, nineteen hundred and thirty-nine
As the Nazi tanks, unopposed, rolled into their town
Rozahn, Poland, my parents (then not yet married) lives were invaded
Fearful, frightened, scared by the realities and all the likelihoods
They headed, by foot, as fast as they could, to the Russian border

That day, they escaped that day, as they gradually made their way
Living by their wits, and the occasional kindnesses of strangers
They got all the way across the border, eventually to Kazakhstan in Russia
And they survived in Kazakhstan, Russia, which became their safe retreat

My father was a tailor with good and proper tailoring skills
They needed tailors in Russia, to manufacture new army uniforms
They conscripted and inducted him, sent him to a (true) labor camp
To work with them, manufacturing many, many Russian army uniforms

I was born in Kazakhstan; I know it sounds exotic; it was just frigid
My mother, her mother (my grandmother) and her young sister (my aunt)
All of us together, banded together for warmth in blankets, with shaking hands
And sometimes freezing toes, and we survived the frigid winters of Kazakhstan, while
Winters, wars and far worse befell the Jews remaining in nearby Poland in those years

We survived and then when the war was finally over, we had a chance to go to America
We arrived in America, a miracle of sorts that we got there when we got there
To the Golden Medina, we took a wetback's papered shortcut guided tour route, we did
I remember the harbor, and seeing the Statue of Liberty pridefully majestically all lit up

"I was only 8" at the time, she writes, they lived in Brooklyn, and she went to school
Optimistically, enthusiastically, as was her father too, looking on the bright side of things
That wasn't possible for her Mom, the years of the Holocaust from 9/1/39 on
Made an indelible, impossible to erase, impression on her psyche and outlook forever

It was hard for her to shake her feelings of alienation, trust was elusive, paranoia reigned
Dad, succeeding in his business, which flourished, could be strong, he could be American
"But, my mother's face showed only dread and grief."
"The trauma of the past years was always as if etched in her psyche"
"Children of Holocaust survivors suffered a subliminal toddler version of those feelings"
Fearful, frightened and scared were we, we are, whenever we contemplate Nazi boots
and swastikas, or any people behaving irrationally, with a venal need to strike at Jews.

December 28, 2020

As a people, we choose, we try to be neighborly and fair, decent and good to get along as long as getting along is reasonably, rationally possible and mutually prescribed. Heaven forbid it would be necessary to choose otherwise.

Genya's story is relevant to the motivation to collect and tell the short stories assembled in this book in much the same way as the stories of Fred and Boris were. After the Holocaust, there was a long period of years that many of us, including among the survivors, had Genya's mother's outlook. They continued to feel alienated from the non-Jewish world and dread and grief with respect to the events during the Holocaust period. We preferred not to discuss them as if those events humiliated us instead of the oppressors who committed the crimes. But overtime, scholarly and academic interest in the events grew. There are more than seventy-five Holocaust museums and memorials in the United States now. There is a general yearning and need for all of us to know more about those events and the people who lived through them. It is, once again, critically important that we do so, given the events that happened at the Capitol Building in Washington, DC, on January 6, 2021.

In recent years, there began a program in the United States called **Witness Theater** in which survivors are grouped and paired with high school students to tell their stories.

Each story was different; each story was the same
They were all about Jews caught in the vise of a viscous international hammerlock
Somehow in some way, those survivors managed to get away, escape
Flee, to be free, from that terrible tyranny, and ultimately land in the U-S of A

An early year of Witness Theater was 2018, seventy-three years after the end of it. The number of survivors, always limited, had dwindled too far too few, and very few of the few had the courage to speak, the stamina to appear, and a voice with which to be heard to recount what happened to them coherently.

Someone had a bright idea, most imaginatively, to bring together
A group of those survivors with some high school students willing to inquire thoughtfully
The students learned firsthand the stories of their elders' survival, escape, arrival
Then, the students were called upon to re-enact a glimpse of it upon a stage

Upon a stage, before an audience, anxious to know and learn about the survivors' lives
There is a common theme: for the survivors, their lives in America were filled with love
Typically, with spouses, children, grandchildren sometimes, all applauding the survivors

Lauding them, remembering the remembrances, first them overcoming the horrors there
Moving in many instances, to almost unimaginable wonderful achievements here.

Witness Theater is a brilliant use of a device to assure the sharing of those remembrances of living survivors telling their stories of escape from the mass murders, slaughterhouse mentality, terrible tragedies, irreplaceable losses, and gross indecencies inflicted on the Jews in Europe during the era of the Holocaust to their victories and decencies in America, Israel, and elsewhere.

Thoughts on Reading This Book

This book similarly consists of some short stories about heroes and heroism during the Holocaust period. These are mostly stories about men and women; a surprising number of very special women who acted heroically during the terrible times—sometimes miraculously—for themselves and, in other instances, completely selfless for the benefit of others. This is not a book best read cover to cover. No, read three stories at a sitting or five at each sitting, perhaps a few more, then take some time to think about the person or persons depicted, the setting, the circumstances, and the outcome. With the benefit of such reflection, draw your own conclusions about the times, the troubles, and the lessons you imagine.

I had control of the computer while this project was ongoing, so I got first crack at selecting the stories, telling the stories, and drawing the points that I deemed to be appropriate. It is not a concession of any kind to acknowledge, as I do, that there are many other stories, many other ways these stories might be told, and many other different valid conclusions and lessons possible to be drawn. Six million Jews died in the Holocaust, and all the survivors were injured or damaged grievously in one way or the other from the actions of an evil empire that began in one of the most cultured, civilized, and well-informed nations on earth. It was an aberration and much worse than merely an aberration. These short stories try to make clear that there were also heroic exceptions.

What the actions of people like Marion Pritchard, George Winton, Hiram Bingham IV, Giorgio Perlasca, Ernst Leitz II, Nancy Grace Augusta Wake Fiocca, Gino Bartali, Irena Sendler, Dr. Adélaïde Hautval, and the others should teach us most of all is that it is, and always was, completely false that "nothing could be done" to stand up for the Jews and others caught in the vise of the killer nightmare, which was Nazism. There were heroes and heroines even within Germany. See "White Roses," "Love Beats Hate on Rosenstrasse," "Picture Perfect," and in Poland. See "The Righteous," "The Priest," and "Garden of Jars," especially. There were whole countries and cultures that stood up for "their" Jews. In Denmark is "Something to Talk About" and Albania is "Cousin Rachel." Bulgaria is a mixed and complicated story, which cuts both ways. See "Uncommon Courage." "Uncommon Courage" is also one of the several involving diplomats who sacrificed their own careers to individually do amazingly unselfish acts. There are examples from Japan, "A Matter of Honor"; Portugal, "Over the Rainbow"; Spain, both "Uncommon Courage" and "Tolerance and Intolerance," and the United States "Heart of Gold." And the surprising results in Italy, then a fascist nation allied with Germany during much of World War II. See "Full Circle,'" "Anonymous," and "Beneath a Scarlet Sky" plus "Award Winner."

There are many instances of Jews acting heroically for themselves starting with Anne Frank and her diary "Saplings from a Chestnut Tree," the Warsaw ghetto fighters in "Fighting for Lost Causes'" and "Vladka's Students," Dr. Janusz Korczak in "Mr. Doctor,'" Boris Kottler in "He Hid in the Woods," and Joseph Moishe Zeller in "Survivor from the Final March." Allied soldiers are the subject of several of the poems from "Our Stars" to "Leaves Quietly Applauding," "Berga und Elster," and finally, most poignantly, "We're All Jews Here."

It is the breadth of the short stories shared that, hopefully, will distinguish this selection. There are proudly stories about righteous individuals recognized in *Yad Vashem* and others about people and events from nowhere near that vicinity. "In the Republic of the Butterflies" honors the unknown many members of the Cultural Council of the Nazi prison camp at Terezín in Czechoslovakia for repairing and cleaning their own water systems and for creating, even in captivity, a place for culture and learning. That story is followed by "Last Year at Marienbad," an ode to a major motion picture rooted in the same geographical area as Terezín with its focus on free will, existentialism, and escapism for all seeking freedom from enforced restrictions.

In "The Greatest Gymnast Ever," the superior story of Agnes Klein Keleti, both a Holocaust survivor and an Olympian gold medalist competing for Hungary in 1956. And "Greedy, Selfish, Bastard," a tin-mining entrepreneur in Bolivia who jumped out of his skin to aid his European fellow Jews to escape to the Americas at risk to his own life and position of privilege and safety in Bolivia when it was a dictatorship.

There are others who crossed lines to do good. Marthe Cohn in "Behind Enemy Lines," an undercover Jewish spy nurse honored even by Germany for nursing German troops while undercover; Giorgio Perlasca in "Award Winner" whose acting performance as a make-believe Spanish diplomat won him the highest honors from Spain; and George Winton in "The White Lion" who used the Kindertransport effort in the UK to save more than 650 children in Prague just before the onset of World War II. Some of those persons have gotten large amounts of public attention. *Remembrances*, this book, tries to make certain that the remembered also include some whose names are almost never mentioned and acts not quite rightly recognized and remain anonymous.

There is Father Pawel Rys in "Why We Remember," Fred Knobloch's Pepo and Mery from "Voices and Echoes," the Polish farmer's wife in "After the Aftermath," Guissippe D'Urso in "Anonymous," Henry Bawnik from "The Cap Arcona," and Marion Pritchard in "A Life Well Spent." This book of remembrances begins with one prose poem about Anne Frank, a name everyone will recognize, and then the one about Marion Pritchard, formerly Marion Phillipina van Binsbergen, whose name almost nobody will recognize and whose brave acts including her pretending to be the unwed birth mother of children with lives at risk simply because they were really Jewish.

The book similarly ends with pieces selected for the contrasts they show: "Tolerance and Intolerance" about four Spanish priests in France who saved some Sephardi "brothers" and the resulting revocation years later of the Edict of Expulsion in Spain in 1992, contrasting with "Pink Graffiti" and the continuation of hateful bigotry even aimed at an honoree as great as Elie Wiesel. There is the blessed brotherhood of Roddie Edmonds ("We're All Jews Here") and, bringing us up to date, the piano-playing open heart, in the midst of the coronavirus pandemic, of Simon Gronowski in Brussels ("Overcoming").

These remembrances are intended to facilitate both remembering the gross criminality and indecency and the overcoming. It is critical for us to understand that not every German was a Nazi, not every Christian was an anti-Semite (indeed some priests, pastors, and nuns died in the camps with us), not every partisan effort was without Jews, and not every Jewish person trapped in the Holocaust surrendered. Many of us overcame and, philosophically, are still overcoming. We are a tiny minority of the population. It is as important today as it ever has been that we recognize that there is a potential for good in people of every faith and nation and risks everywhere of civilizations going off the tracks ("Adelaide, the Saint").

We can all be brothers and sisters with the capacity to be united by common principles of decency and humanity. "Hope Is the Last to Die" is as true for all of us as it was for Helene Birenbaum. Think, if you will, of the representatives and senators in the United States Congress Capitol Building hiding and huddling in fear for their lives on January 6, 2021. How close were they to an incident of mass assassination? No nation has an absolute monopoly on the ability to distinguish justice from injustice as was shown by Hans Scholl and his sister Sophie in "White Roses." And in the depths of Auschwitz where an unknown German engineer was able to teach Gene Klein the basic principles of humanity ("Guiding Principles"). This little book hopes to be an eye-opening experience permitting readers to draw their own lessons from the Holocaust.

Remembrances, we are required to remember and never to forget. The whole entire world is required to remember and never forget. It is possible to fight hate and injustice by seeking justice, evenly applied, and to help bring about a more amazing and honorable world by chipping in, contributing with acts thoughtfully. Who is the question? Everyone is the answer. All of us.

don david Calderon y. Aroesty

Credits

In any piece of creative writing, the responsibility for errors or omissions is solely on the author. That said, *Remembrances* would not have been possible for me to write without the efforts and contributions of others; all of whom deserve valuable credit and honorable mention for their assistance. Thank you:

- **Alex Close. The illustrations included in this volume are the creation of Ms. Alex Close. Alex is a Canadian visual artist and researcher who took BFA at OCAD University (Canada, 2015), MLitt, fine art at Glasgow School of Art (UK, 2017), and MDes at Carleton University (Canada, 2020). Alex is also proud of her Macedonian heritage.**
- **Gabby Flamm. Gabrielle is a Holocaust scholar with a bachelor's degree from West Chester University of Pennsylvania, focusing on Holocaust and genocide studies; United States teaching assistant with Fulbright Austria; currently studying for a master's degree in Southeastern European Studies at KT Karl Frazens Universitat in Graz, Austria.**
- **Dr. Sofija Grandakovska. Associate professor at City University of New York's John Jay College of Criminal Justice and Anthropology Department in comparative literature and interdisciplinary studies in Holocaust, Jewish history, literature, and culture.**

The contributions of the three young women are all very important. One does not properly measure the power of an ocean by any one wave, and yet without each wave contributing to the continuation of the flow, the ocean would be without direction and powerless. Never underestimate the value of observations and assistance in scholarship.

My wife, Michelle Nash Cohen, it takes great patience and much love to sustain any marriage of more than fifty-six years. I more than used up my reasonably allocated share of her patience and love during those decades and especially in the course of the writing endeavors following a cardiac arrest on September 21, 2012. Due credit is the least of my debt.

My creative writing tutors and classmates at LIU's adult education programs at Hutton House, especially under the guidance of a prescient writer/ghostwriter Ms. Lisa Pulitzer and those with me in Lisa's classes offering understanding and encouragement.

The survivors that I have personally known and implicitly credit in *Remembrances* and friends who are survivors: Boris Kottler, Fred Knobloch, and Regina Pearlman. Also, I am thankful to multiple friends who graciously provided good cheer and emotional support along the way, especially but not only Dr. Bert Kohn and Mr. William Lang.

Dr. Grandakovska's scholarly achievements and literary accomplishments far exceeding the scope of this small volume and included her service as a postdoctoral fellow at Yad Vashem in Jerusalem, Israel, and as a visiting scholar at the Center for Jewish History in New York City.

Her kind consideration of this work is very much appreciated.

List of Remembrances

Volume 1

Volume 2

Volume 3

BUTTERFLIES

VOLUME 1

Remembrances

Remembering
We are enjoined to remember
And, never to forget
Things we did not know then
Mostly, we do not know now
And, cannot even quite imagine

These poems are dedicated
Dedicated to those events
To the duty we freely undertake
To honor the memories of millions
Of mostly unknown victims, by identifying
Some heroes, heroines and gratifying events

The world will never be, never be
A blank page on which to start anew
History is a very tall waterfall
Replenishing and redirecting the waters
From the deeply rooted routes of the past
To the rushing rivers of the future, unforeseen

Remembrances, these and many others, are required reading
If there's to be any chance, any chance at all
To change what was to what can possibly be
Profitably and prophetically determined to be
A safe and sound, and entirely reasonable, hopeful
Responsible new direction for the world, for you and me.

September 2017

President Dwight David Eisenhower
When he was commander in chief
Of all the allied forces
The victorious allied forces, warned us

Uncovering the horrors
Of the concentration camps
Discovering the dead and barely living

Eisenhower demanded that we take pictures
Photographs to record the actual facts
That it happened, beyond deniability

These remembrances are meant to be
Mental photographs
Recorded with words and phrases
We are enjoined to remember
And never to forget, never to forget
That there were also heroes and heroines
Exhibiting gumption, selflessness, care and concern

This universe will never be all it can ever be
Unless the heroes and the heroines are applauded
And emulated—in every context everywhere
There are recognizable forces for decency and justice
In every contest and context in all of life's theaters
Remembrances seek to avoid such bravery disappearing.

In the 21st Century, streets are again occasionally littered with swastikas
Synagogue windows smashed as if the shards of glass were meaningless
The entire European continent seeming to be lapsing into collective amnesia
Beat, Drag and Suffocate, a rallying cry for know-nothings of many persuasions
Too few who dare to elevate decency, justice and fairness over all concerns

Those who fail to study history
Or who report it inaccurately
Are condemned, condemn us all
To repetitions of history's mistakes

D. David Cohen, Roslyn, NY,
Written in his Sephardic family names
Adopted pen name for all the Remembrances
And certain other observations

don david Calderon y. Aroesty

Saplings from a Chestnut Tree

This is a story which is continuing
It was not finished then; it is not finished now
Born in Frankfurt, Germany
In Nineteen Hundred and Twenty-Nine
Annaliese Marie Frank might have
Passed through life, unnoticed
As many and most persons do
If things had only been different

But, they were not different, the Nazis
First gained control of Germany in 1933
Desperate, and not waiting for the storm
To gather steam, her father moved the family
The whole entire family, to Amsterdam
The Netherlands, but by 1940
The Nazis occupied The Netherlands as well
From '42 to '44, Anne kept a diary, daily notes

While hiding in a concealed room
Behind a bookcase in the building
Where her father had once worked
Hiding with the consent and participation
Of some brave and special Dutch people
Still, they could not hide forever
Two long years, two very long years in hiding
The Nazis arrested the Frank family in August of '44

They could not outlast the spreading storm
The Nazis sent Anne and her sister to Bergen Belsen
A German concentration camp in Saxony, Germany
She passed in February or March, of 1945
She was survived by her diaries
Saved and retained by one of her family's Dutch helpers
Published, in Dutch, in 1947
And then translated, and republished in more than 60 languages

The Holocaust deniers deny
The Holocaust deniers deny the concentration camps

The Holocaust deniers deny the camps were used
As mechanized killing machines, to eliminate the innocent
The Holocaust deniers deny Zyklon B, it did not exist
Was not used, millions were not rounded up, captured
Sent to the showers, gassed and incinerated, or killed
By many other means, including starvation and intentional neglect

The Holocaust deniers deny
That Annaliese Marie Frank ever existed
That she, a teenage girl, could have written it
That she wrote it, in those cramped quarters
That her diary was her diary, written and maintained
By her, and is, a valuable and to-be valued insight
Into the capacity of man's inhumanity to man
Or simply to the mindset and suffering of those hiding in a closet

She wrote her dairies to a fictional friend, Kitty, by name
She disclosed her secrets only to the diary, there were no other
No other intended readers then, she was alone with her thoughts
Her fears, regrets, observations and, dare she believe in them, hopes
Subdued imagined notions that the world might again become
Become a better place, but she herself did not live to see the peace
The entirety of her diary was written without her having the benefit of sunlight
From the darkened, dampened sequestered quarters of their self-confinement

Outside of the building in which they were encamped
There was, she saw and much admired, a horse chestnut tree
When, years long after the war, the chestnut tree was failing
Saplings from it were distributed and supplied to others
Followers of the Anne Frank history and the story in her diary
So that additional chestnut trees might grow from the saplings
And so it is, as well, that we tell, the Anne Frank history and the story in her diary
That young ladies, and other citizens of the world, may grow from knowing it

May 18, 2017

In addition to Anne Frank and her sister, Margot
More than One Million Jewish children perished in the Holocaust
Their memories must always be cherished, remembered respectfully
That is the point, the principal, principled point, of *Yad Vashem*
And other Holocaust Museums and places of remembrance
Innocents and innocence were trampled, crushed and turned to dust
Solely because of, for no other reason, our race, religion, and godliness

A Life Well Spent

Sometimes, there are times
I like to read obituaries
Of lives well spent and otherwise
Marion Phillippina van Binsbergen
Was born in Amsterdam, the Netherlands
In Nineteen Hundred and Twenty
Her father was a Dutch Judge
Her mother, an Englishwoman, an Anglican
Her upbringing was a good and proper one
As a young woman, she had many friends
And good relationships with her neighbors
She was raised in the Anglican Christian faith
Instilled with a sense of justice and morality
Correctness, knowing the difference between
Right and wrong; she needed to know the difference

The German Nazis invaded the Netherlands
In Nineteen Hundred and Forty
Her father, the Judge, hated Nazi ideology
Marion was a university student, trying
Trying to live life normally in the midst
Of occupation, disruption and deportations
Trying to live normally, while knowing
The difference between right and wrong
Bicycling to school one day, on a street nearby
A street she knew from the day she was mobile
She saw Nazi soldiers and hooligans
Picking up little children by their pigtails
Or their limbs, and throwing them in a truck
The liquidation of a Jewish home for children
Just part of the process of mass deportation

The Anglican in her clicked in, and there would be no more
No more living life normally, as it had once been
With the assistance of neighbors and friends, many of them
Marion became a savior, saving dozens of them
Spiriting some to safe houses, hiding others under floor boards
She created a network, to feed, to clothe, to hide away many,

Perhaps as many as 150 people, hiding from the Nazi dragnet
She got them false identification papers, scrounged extra
Ration cards, recruited and trained host families to take them in
Prepared the families for the perils they, and she, faced
The toughness of the tasks, notwithstanding, she was committed
To fighting persecution, to combating against intolerant indignities

In the Netherlands, with the Dutch resistance, for the free Dutch
She made her parents proud, her nation proud, later, recognized
At *Yad Vashem*, as one of the "Righteous among the nations"
She was surely, certainly, a righteous woman
A righteous Christian Anglican woman, a star
A bright star who sparkled best when the world was dark
She married an American GI and became an American too
She walked and worked among us, quiet about her heroism
Marion Pritchard's star dimmed on December 11, 2016
In Washington, DC, United States of America
She left three natural born children, eight grandchildren
and one great grandson
She also leaves innumerable others elsewhere on Earth
Children of the children she personally saved in the Netherlands
Including those she saved by her merciful "missions of disgrace"
When she pretended to be the unwed mother of babies
Babies born of Dutch Jewish parents, who needed to hide
Hide infants from the grasping arms of Nazi death machines
Marion knew the difference, the difference between right and wrong.

December 21, 2016

In her life well spent
She also shot and killed a Dutch policeman
A Dutch policeman cooperating with the Nazis
There, threatening to turn in a family of four
Who'd been hiding beneath the floor boards
She was always bothered by it; but it had to be done
It had to be done, there was no choice, because
The butchering of innocents could simply not be undone.

The White Lion

Rescinding his conscientious objections
Bravely, he served as a flight officer
During WWII, in the Royal Air Force
He received no special medals or commendations
Nobody knew then what he had done before the war began

His parents were German Jews at the turn of the century
Before WWI, they moved to London, it was 1907
His father was Rudolph Wertheim, a bank manager
His mother, Barbara, had a maiden name of Wertheimer

Wertheim and Wertheimer, Germans, became English
Jews, they then converted faithfully to the Christian religion
Their son, Nicholas George, was born in 1909, and baptized
Soon after, they changed the family name to Winton

Their transformation was complete, no longer German
No longer Jewish, no longer Wertheim, they were
Officially, unofficially, divorced from who they'd been
They had no named ties to anything German, anyone Jewish

The troubles started more than twenty years later
Hitler first became the Chancellor in 1933
Soon, Jews living in Germany could no longer do so safely
And in 1938, English people of every faith reached out

They extended their arms and opened their homes
In an unprecedented program called *Kindertransport*
To provide a place to live for Jewish children at risk, initially
they took those without parents, without homes, without food

Those were the priorities, in fact, all the Jewish children
within reach of Nazis and Nazism were severely at risk
The first *Kindertransport* arrived in Harwick, England
In December of 1938, 200 orphans from an orphanage
An orphanage which had been destroyed on *Kristillnacht*

Additional children followed from many places, cities
Such as Berlin, Vienna, Prague and other cultural gems
Where Jewish life and Jewish lives were disappearing
The efforts to save the children were truly miraculous

English Jews, Quakers and Christians of all denominations
Were required to work together, pull together, and pray
The route for the Kindertransports was arduous, trains to
Belgium or the Netherlands, boats from there to England
While, even prior to September 1, 1939, Nazis were lurking
There are many stories about those *Kindertransports*
And the thousands of children saved by those maneuvers
Starting with the courage of the parents to let them go
And the sacrifices of the English to take them in, to provide
Safe refuge for strangers, many of whom spoke not one English word

Those stories are emotional, heart wrenching, almost unbelievable
Tales of heroes and heroism, from the leaders of the movement
In Germany and in England, to the volunteers on both sides
The children who saw it through and, of course, their foster families
But, perhaps, there is no story more dramatic than that of George Winton

You remember Nicholas George, the child of Rudolph and Barbara Winton
He was kind of a *bon vivant* in England, he had first attended public school
Failed, left without qualifications, attending instead night school while
Working for banks, in England, then Germany, France and back to London

He was a stock broker on the London Stock Exchange
And an accomplished athletic fencer, intending to compete in the Olympics
Though the 1940 Olympics never happened, they were cancelled by the war
In 1938, Christmas time, the 29-year-old bachelor had planned to vacation
To vacation in Switzerland, when he was diverted, diverted to Prague

In Prague for many weeks, he rolled up his sleeves, and became a one-man band
Playing an incessant tune, demanding, insisting, arranging *Kindertransports*
For the Czech children, mostly, not all, Jews, at risk from the German take over
As the German occupation and stranglehold of Czechoslovakia was completed

Though he, himself, never set foot in Prague's railway station, it became the central meeting point and send
    off place for each group of Czech kids getting out of there, away from the certain path of harm's way
    George Winton organized and managed everything, the lists, the trains, the boats
From the track of their departure to the port of their safe arrival in England
In all, from December of 1938 to the last week of August in 1939, nine months
George Winton successfully arranged for 669 Czech children to get out of there
Away from the conflict, away from the war, out of the grasp of Nazi predators

For fifty years, no one took note of this, announced it, published it
Recognized the enormity of George Winton's achievements, with the help of others
Many others, George, self-effacing as he was, always remembered the many others
It was already 1988, when the story was finally fully told, and the honors were bestowed
Among other things, Queen Elizabeth made him English royalty, and
In the Czech Republic, the President inducted him into the Order of the White Lion.

October 30, 2017

There are ironies in this story too
George Winton could not be recognized in Yad Vashem
In the hall of the Righteous Heroes, because, because
According to them, calculating as they do, he was a Jew
Born of a Jewess, Barbara Winton, born Wertheimer
Notwithstanding her total transformation after 1907
And the Baptism of the baby, Nicholas George
Christian upbringing, Christian learning and beliefs
Could not, did not, shake off her or his Jewishness
Hitler and his Nazi theologians would agree with that
George, himself, tired of all religions religious claims of right
He'd witnessed both sides in WWII claiming God's support
He chose "ethics" as the code of conduct for him to follow
White Lions are not a separate breed
They are just the same as all the others
Except when they have good cause to roar
They roar exceptionally; they stand out, outstandingly

WHITE LION IN PRAGUE

Her Middle Name Was Sara

She, I imagine, in my mind's eye
Had blond hair, with lots of curls
When she was just a little girl
When she was just a little girl
And, blue, blue eyes with a twinkle
She liked to ride her three-wheeler
And, jump up in Daddy's arms
That was only one of her many charming
Ways; there were multiple other things
The way she feigned to dance ballet
And, curtsied as if to the opera's audience
The way she mimicked Mama
Especially, in the kitchen, cooking
Up a storm of dirty pots and pans
And, who could ever forget, if ever
Her sitting on Granpapa's lap
Tweaking with his Van Dyke beard
Laughing aloud, with each pinch and twist

It was a perfect picture of perfection
In Nineteen Hundred and Thirty-Five
In Vienna, the most cosmopolitan of cities
Among the grandest places you'd ever
Seek to visit, a pleasant place of pleasure
Although a boiling pot of assassination and intrigue
Before the *Anschluss*, reunification with Germany
Willing surrender to Hitler and fascist Nazi theology

After surrender, her middle name was Sara or Sarah
The spelling did not matter; every Jewess knew now
She had a middle name of Sara, to keep it always
All her life, forever, though it wasn't very long
She died in eastern Poland, a remote camp
In Nineteen Hundred and Forty-Two
She was innocent and sweet, kind and good
Timid and fearful; there came a time when
She'd never laugh again, the emotional pain
Was just unthinkable, unbearable, incessant

Previously, she had liked to ride her tricycle
And play with Granpapa's Van Dyke beard
That made her an enemy, an enemy of the state
Someone the big brave Nazis simply had to liquidate
Make disappear, with each and every Sara in their sphere

2014

Visiting Vienna, the most cosmopolitan of cities
There is so much to see and love, the sites are bright
And plentiful, there are many things to easily enjoy
But, the visit would be less than complete
Without remembering Sara or Sarah,
Every Jewish girl in Hitler's Nazi world
Had to forever be known also as Sara or Sarah

Saved by Jerusalem

He was one of too few who were enabled
Able to get away from Nazi occupied Austria
When getting away was feasible but where-to-go was not
Before the Holocaust ravaged almost all who, stuck—there, remained

Music was not only his vocation
His piano skills proved to be his passport
He earned an exit visa, an opportunity to play
To play with, and for, the Jerusalem conservatory
Jerusalem, in Palestine, before the war

Palestine was controlled by the British then
And, notwithstanding the circumstances
In Germany, Austria, the Czech Republic, and
All the places where the Jewish world was already burning
Jewish entry into Palestine was still strictly regulated and limited by the Brits

Before there was any certain knowledge of the final solution
They could not be teachers; they could not be students
They would not be left alone, even in their own hometowns
They were not permitted to be human, human beings
There was an awful stench and evil premonitions in the air

The sparks of anti-Semitism once ignited and fanned
Spread quickly and harshly, burning indiscriminately
Not confined by any borders or natural barriers
Walter Hautzig was luckily enabled by his musical talents
To leave the sparking all-consuming fire in Europe, and get away to Jerusalem

Eventually, he reunited with his family in America,
Became an American; married a Russian Jewish lady
Together, they became just another American family
An American family indirectly saved by the existence of Jerusalem
Before Jerusalem was the capital of Israel, before the State existed

On the piano, Walter Hautzig enthusiastically played
Played all of the keys; he loved to harmonize, a professor of piano,
At the Peabody Conservatory in Baltimore; a living proponent of

His contention that all music is nonsectarian, classical music appeals
Universally, especially, to the tastes of thinking believing human beings

Later, much later, he would be quoted as saying
That the music of Beethoven and Chopin is as good
"For the Jews as it is for the gentiles"
He refused, however, to play their music
To a racially segregated audience in 1940s Alabama

He played all the keys, he was inclusive
For the ebony and the ivory, before others knew
Music is not ever, never exclusionary, he believed
Walter Hautzig passed away quietly early in 2017
He had been saved by Jerusalem to help bring harmony to America

don david Calderon y. Aroesty
February 4, 2017

Walter Hautzig experienced Vienna at its best, then barely escaped it, at its worst
There are borders for reasons and reasonable, responsible requirements
He did not, never did, suggest any immigration expertise, still we all know
Instinctively know, that closing the doors of America
To the world's most hungry and needy truly seeking peace and freedom
Seems antithetical to this nation's finest principles and greatest hopes
Walter Hautzig is a reminder and a symbol. for the best we can be
Walter Hautzig, an immigrant American, loved to harmonize

In the Republic of the Butterflies

He was too old to serve in World War I
He had been born in his country and lived there all of his life
Until he was sent, at age 58, to the area, later known as
The Republic of the Butterflies

When he first arrived, even when he first arrived
It was old and dirty, the streets were cobblestone,
Difficult to walk upon, there were rats, many rats and other insects
The human population was initially disproportionately the elderly

There were some families, entire families, but mostly the elderly
And other persons of "special merit," selected and singled out
There were thousands, even in the beginning, and the population grew
Almost as if it were a booming town, at least 50,000, maybe as many as 75,000

There were counts, attendance counts, and census taking daily, regularly
It was formerly a fortress erected outside of Prague, in what was then Slovakia
Constructed in the years between 1780 and 1790, and said to have been
Designed by an Emperor to be part of a projected fort system for the entirety

In its inception, it was grand and grandiose; one could still see evidence of that
In the sculptures, in the intricate design of some of the building walls,
In the high ceilings; but the whole system of fortifications was never completed
And, the facilities were allowed to decay, become obsolete and mostly useless.

Little attention was paid to maintenance or refurbishment, a small part of it
had been made into a prison, the prison was used, among other things,
To house the assassin who fired the shots which caused the start of WWI
Now, in WWII, it was suddenly a home for thousands of displaced innocents

They were there awaiting relocation, relocation to nowhere,
It was represented to be a "model" camp, but the barracks were skimpy,
Rooms insufficient, the number of beds less than 1 per person,
The toilets inadequate and malfunctioning for some time, medical care was lacking

There was rampant malnutrition and disease, inadequate response to those conditions
A Cultural Council was formed, an effort at least at self-governance, the Council

undertook to revamp the water supply entirely, the residents dug up all the old pipes
Reinstalled completely cleansed pipes in a new aquatic system with drinkable water

The population became more mixed; more children from many countries
The children needed to be educated, they were home schooled, read books, wrote poetry
And they drew pictures, many pictures, some of them quite artistic, both the artistic ones
And some of the others, have been saved as remembrances, many remembrances

The Council arranged for plentiful cultural activities with lectures, recitals, poetry
Readings, and concerts, four orchestras were formed; there was chamber music,
Jazz ensembles too, stage performances were produced, directed and performed
Many prominent artists lived for a short while in the Republic of the Butterflies

There were writers, scientists, jurists, diplomats, musicians and scholars.
They even produced a Cultural Council magazine called *Vedem*
The Vedem world was both real and make-believe; it was like waking up to sunshine
Knowing that before the sun would set, some fraction of the population would disappear,
Never to be seen again, transported to nowhere, before the setting sun had set

How does one possibly yearn for the sun to rise again, or manage the courage
To participate, as artist or audience member, in the next day's cultural events
When some fraction of the population would daily disappear, never to be seen again
This was the Nazi concentration camp known as Terezín, in the Czech Republic,
From November 24, 1941 to liberation, by advancing Soviet troops, on May 8, 1945

don david Calderon y. Aroesty, 2015

The Republic of the Butterflies, is the name of the book
The book written by the Italian author, Matteo Corradini
With the history of the magazine, *Vedem*
The book was read aloud by Ben Kingsley on January 27, 2015
At Thereinstadt, where Terezín was located
For the commemoration of International Holocaust Day

Last Year at Marienbad

In the stone and marble gardens of Marienbad
A butterfly flitters and flies beautifully, existentially
The butterfly has no certain knowledge of right and wrong
The butterfly only knows she'll not be there for long

Brightly dressed and colored, she draws attention everywhere
Especially here, in the black and white of Marienbad
She flies to seduce, induce, the chase to follow
Careful to avoid, evade, her capture, now or in the morrow

Marienbad is the perfect setting for this clever plot
Bohemia, Slovakia, part Czech, part German
Literally, in Slovakian, the name means beautiful spa park
During the war just ended, the scene near Marienbad was very dark

Now, see the romantic pillars, extraordinary historical sculptures,
So many places to play hide and seek, seek and hide again
Charming pavilions, the hoi polloi of the hoi polloi, enjoying
The fresh mountain forest air, and the therapeutic heated springs

The butterfly returns with her beautiful large feminine wings
She smiles, coyly, quietly, says "do not bother me"
At the same time she oozes sensuality, at the same time
She has the ability to disguise herself plainly, a leaf in the bark of a tree

She's free, from predators, they're all predators, with their ties and nets
She's capable of extraordinary transformations, a metamorphosis
Suspended by her silken threads, she sheds the skin with which she came
She knows who she is, revealing sensuous new skin, assuming self-responsibility

Existentially, it is the plight of the individual, always, to exercise free will
The butterfly can stay or leave, leave or stay, capable also of migrating
To avoid adverse conditions, escape from the grasp of hostile others
This is the butterfly's newfound principle, it is me, myself, on whom she must rely

That cannot be denied; in every ending to this play, free will triumphs
Only a generation before 1961, millions mindlessly abandoned choice
To swear undying loyalty and allegiance to some ism other than existentialism

When at the essence of all existence, even the butterflies.
Even, the female butterflies, have rights to self determination
Liberty and freedom, *Vedem*, cultural self-expressionism.

March 13, 2014

During the war just ended, the scene near Marienbad was very dark
Literally, in Slovakian, the name means beautiful spa park
Existential escapism, survival first and then self-determination
Liberty and freedom, *Vedem*, self-expression, as a means to an end

To those trapped in the grip of the Holocaust
***Vedem*, self-expression, was a thin rope of hope for them**
Grasping and grappling with the awful circumstances
Working and praying for any possibility of sunlight opening up their lives
Last year at Marienbad was a motion picture, not necessarily
Intended to be taken literally, nor to be interpreted only in one specific way
Importantly, the lead, a symbol for all females. had the ability and the guile to be
A leaf in the bark of a tree; during WWII, we all sought to be nimble like butterflies

Heart of Gold

Someone later said he had "a heart of gold"
Perhaps, he did, but what he did, we did not know of it, until recently
Hiram Bingham, the Fourth, was made from prime stock
His mother was a Tiffany, brilliant and a gem of a person too
His father was Hiram Bingham III, an archeologist of some repute
An Indiana Jones character, who made a significant discovery

When the ancient Inca city of Machu Picchu was thought to be lost forever
Hiram Bingham III uncovered it, in Peru, in 1911, and he publicized the discovery
Arranged for trains to be built to bring the tourists there, where later it was
Recognized to be, one of the seven man-made wonders of the world, a unique place
The Fourth was only eight then, when Daddy's reputation was lighting up
Later, Hiram Bingham III became the Governor of Connecticut, then a US Senator

The Fourth was much less pretentious, and not as outstanding as his father
He had attended Groton Academy and then Yale, Class of 1925
He chose, for his career, to be in the United States Foreign Service
He served well and loyally in various places, including Japan and China
A diplomat, a junior consular officer stationed in France, in 1940

It was only months after the fall of France and the survival of Vichy France,
Barely surviving, Vichy had agreed to turn over immediately on demand, any refugees
Any refugees from Nazi Germany sought by Nazi Germany, the victors in the war
The war just fought was hardly fought; one million Frenchmen had died in WWI
They weren't repeating that endeavor, this time they caved and surrendered, for peace

The peace they got was hardly honorable; one would not reasonably call it that
It was a back of the alley arrangement between the aggressors and the assaulted
Half of France, including Paris and the Atlantic coast, would be German Army occupied
The other half of France, the southern part, touching on the Mediterranean
That would be self-governed, self-governed mostly by Petain's toothless tigers

That's the place Fourth found himself, based in Marseilles with instructions
Instructions from Washington to do nothing to upset the balance of power
No extra visas, no speed up in processing, nothing to change what was happening
One had to be blind not to see what was happening; the night had descended in France
To the artists, the actors, the poets, writers, Jews, everyone who opposed Nazism

Soon would be subject to arrest, imprisonment, and eventually elimination, being erased
Erased was a polite way of describing the political plague which was rapidly spreading
Spreading over all of Europe; Harry Bingham IV would not be part of that, he stood out
He worked with Varian Fry, another brave American who brought himself to be there
In the middle of the fight, for the benefit of the Emergency Rescue Committee
And a rag tag team of very few others to try to save a few, that's all that they could do

To save a few, maybe 2,000 of them, including Marc Chagall, Max Ernst, Hannah Arendt
And miscellaneous unknown, untalented, nobody ever heard of them, people
Not only Jews, there were some Christian German refugees from Hitler's Nazism too
Bingham was essential to the operation, only he had the capacity to write visas, expedite
Cases, that's what he did do, more than that, he took risks with his personal life safety

For all his good deeds, he was demoted and transferred; official Washington disapproved
But before he was demoted, transferred and shipped to South America anonymously
To continue in foreign service as an unknown nobody himself, there was Feuchtwanger
Lion Feuchtwanger was a German who read *Mein Kampf*, when it was first published
Before Adolf Hitler was Adolf Hitler, *Fürher* of the German Reich, and a potentate
And Lion had written a review which said that *Mein Kampf* had 140,000 words,
140,000 mistakes; so after Hitler was empowered, Feuchtwanger quickly ran to France

The Reich forces relished the thought of capturing him in Vichy
He was briefly caught, briefly interred; Harry Bingham IV personally set him free
Housed him, fed him, saved his soul and energy, until Feuchtwanger could walk away
He walked across the Pyrenees to safe harbor in Spain and eventual escape to the US

Lion Feuchtwanger, the German Jewish novelist, playwright and essayist was saved,
Settled in California, granted asylum, thanks entirely to Harry Bingham's courage
And generosity, nothing could be more generous than reaching out, risking everything
For strangers in desperate need of escape from monsters with insatiable appetites.

March 21, 2017

During World War II
In the face of Nazi tyranny
The US Department of State
Made a callously self-interested decision
It officially discouraged our diplomats from helping refugees
They officially were ordered to show little flexibility and no compassion
Even for what were considered the most deserving and desperate refugees
Some blame instinctive anti-Semitism, not hating Jews specifically
Just a polite, realistic, reckoning that it would be impossible to take them all
Why possibly try to pick and choose, discriminating, no doubt, unlawfully

Harry Bingham's courage and capacity was mostly unknown to the world
Until many years later, after his death in 1988, at age 85

He had saved the records from his time in the Foreign Service in Marseilles
They were unearthed from his family farm in Connecticut
Long lost records discovered, like Machu Picchu, in Peru, had been uncovered
And they confirmed the facts; that Harry had done what he had done
He has recently been recognized for his courage and capacity, true American grit
Rules are rules for reasons; nothing is more courageous than breaking broken rules.

The Yellow Star

The dim yellow star was forced on us
Rammed down our throats
The ones who created it, intended
That it stand for dishonor
An admission of guilt
For the crime of being Jewish

A dreary cloth patch
In the shape of the Star of David
Every German Jew was required to wear one
Then, as the Nazi military conquered countries
The Jews in each and every conquered entity
They, too, had to display the yellow badge

Mostly, European non-Jews stood by
They watched the phenomenon
And marveled at the German efficiency
Some even allied openly with Germany
Others craved independence from Nazism
But not at the price of defending their Jews

The yellow star is a testament
To all who died tragically wearing it
Rather than dishonor, it is a symbol
Of honor and pride, a refusal to abandon faith
The insistence that there is a God, one God
Who helps us all, every one of us, to serve faithfully.

December 29, 2016

With credit to Dr. Chaim Bernard, Tel-Aviv
Who wrote a letter to the Editor, *The New York Times*
European edition, with many of these words and phrases
A number of years ago, after the Boston Marathon bombing

This week, the Obama Administration engineered
And then refused to veto, a resolution at the Security Council
Of the United Nations, to condemn Jewish Settlements
In East Jerusalem and in areas of the West Bank

Tagging us, if you will, with another yellow star
Let's call it what it was, Anti-Israeli anti-Semitism
Masked as a pathetic lame duck attempt to stimulate
Peace discussions with adversaries who want no peace with Israel.

WHITE ROSES

HEADLESS NAZI OPERATING GUILLOTINE

Over the Rainbow

Once upon a time, long ago, Portugal had a plentiful and prospering Jewish population
That was when Spain, Portugal's next door neighbor, kicked out all of its Jews, in 1492
King John of Portugal failed and refused to follow suit; he preferred to keep the Jews
But only five years later, the new King of Portugal wanted to marry Princess Isabella
the daughter of King Ferdinand and Queen Isabella of Spain, and for the love
Of his life and a perfect royal match, in 1497, Portugal also expelled the Jews

Four Hundred and Forty Three years after the Portuguese expulsion,
The Jews, running from the rest of Europe, were left with few choices
As to where to go, anywhere to go, and all that was open to them were those
Few choices, the neutral countries, neither aligned with Germany nor against it
Sweden, Switzerland, Spain and Portugal were the European alternatives in 1940
For a stateless Jew, getting a visa to one of those countries was darn near impossible

Without crossing an ocean, they needed a miracle, a place and a way over the rainbow
Aristides de Sousa Mendes was a consul general for Portugal in Bordeaux, France
Germany invaded France; in the Spring of 1940, France was seeking a peace pact
Everyone who was anyone knew with a certainty that the pact would not be evenhanded
There were going to be provisions requiring France to surrender, and to surrender Jews
Tens of thousands of Jewish refugees had descended on Bordeaux by June, 1940

According to historians, Aristides de Sousa Mendes offered to help those refugees
Initially, he offered to help a single family, a Polish Rabbi, Chaim Kruger, and family
After Sousa Mendes's applications to Portugal for the Krugers were denied,
Sousa Mendes decided to risk his life and whole career, he promised to help them himself
Fact or fable tell us that Kruger unselfishly asked not only for himself and his family
He plead instead for all of the Jews caught in Bordeaux, with their lives in danger

Sousa Mendes determined to act, would not refuse to act, fail to be of assistance
He chose instead, in lieu of compliance with the Portuguese rules and regulations
To himself issue Portuguese visas to each and every applicant who made it to his office
At least 30,000 applicants made it to his office, and 30,000 visas were issued by him
In direct contravention of the orders from the dictator, then dictating what to do
Sousa Mendes had those orders, and chose, for no personal benefit, to defy them

As if intending to make matters worse for himself, Sousa Mendes defiantly led a caravan
A caravan of mostly stateless Jewish refugees, to a little known outpost in the Pyrenees
Where they could depart directly from Vichy France to enter Spain en route to Portugal

The Portuguese foreign minister wasted no time, no time at all, firing him
Sousa Mendes spent the next decade, the rest of his life, shunned, unemployed,
Unemployable, and in dire personal financial straits, until he died in 1954
For standing by his principles, Sousa Mendes was turned into a blacklisted, broken man
After the war, the Holocaust was exposed, and Portugal took credit for saving those Jews
Memories of Sousa Mendes long forgotten, he got neither credit nor compensation for it.

March 11, 2019

Doing the right and proper thing
Does not always end up being recognized
And sometimes ends up being penalized
No one knows for sure his or her personal motivation
But we all know, should know, that Aristides de Sousa Mendes
Acted exceptionally bravely for Portugal, when Portugal
and those refugees most needed his exceptional bravery

Rabbi Kruger may have acted heroically too
He could have asked only for himself
But when he plead, he plead instead
For everyone caught in the same plight
He made it possible for Sousa Mendes to see the light
Unselfishness breeds additional unselfishness

Somewhere over the rainbow was a song written before the war
But for the refugee Jews caught in the vise of Vichy France
In 1940, while the Nazis and the collaborators ruled, it was prophetic
The troubled skies in Europe were full of dark clouds and little hope
Aristides de Sousa Mendes rose to the challenge of the times, thanks to him
Somewhere over the rainbow, bluebirds did fly away from the turmoil
With their Portuguese visas held high, the dreams they dreamed of
Escape, safe passage, revival, renewal, sometimes dreams do come true

White Roses

Even in Germany during WWII
Even in the heart of the boiling cauldron
Amidst the heated fury and persistent hate
A flickering white light of hope and humanity

The evidence of it was barely seen or sensed
Underreported, believed to be nonexistent
Their world was entirely black and red
Swastikas spreading throughout Europe

Few dared to imagine white roses
Poetic words advancing a strong moral compass
Pointing in an entirely different direction
Rejecting meandering acts of shameful infamy

Who were they, those Germans with white roses?
College students, idealists, common sense philosophers
Innocents acting innocently
They plotted secretly, almost irreverently

They confronted murder and mayhem
With words as swords in published leaflets
Imploring the public to a passive resistance
They employed neither bullets nor bombs

Decency, they called for decency
Honesty, straightforwardness
"Every word that comes from Hitler's mouth
Is a lie," they asserted: "We will not be silent"

But, in the end, they were silenced
Their heads were chopped off
By Nazis using a guillotine
In February of 1943

February of 1943 was still the beginning
Still the beginning of the march to madness
Defeat at Stalingrad caused no serious reassessment
Denial and darkness covered up the folly of German Fascism

That denial and misguided patriotism crippled all
the remaining White Rose adherents, just as
A curtain was closing on an entire continent
Some, too few, remember the courage and the selflessness
Of the martyrs and the message of the White Rose

February 22, 2018 (the seventy-fifth annual commemorative)

Hans Scholl, his sister, Sophie
Alexander Schmorell
Christoph Probst, Will Graf
Less well-known and anonymous to others
Inspired by the sermons of
The Lion of Munster, the right and
Catholic, Bishop Clemens August von Galen
They, too, resisted the Holocaust
Not only for right, plain as black and white
Nor for any ulterior motives
But for Germany, they wanted
Germany to be the best it could be
Every nation, every group, everywhere
Needs skeptics carrying white roses
Dissent can be the most patriotic patriotism

Love Beats Hate on Rosenstrasse

Rosenstrasse is the name of the street where a collective street protest did happen
A collective street protest which took place in Berlin, Germany, February/March 1943
During the height of Nazi power, and in the middle of the wars,
A protest by the non-Jewish wives of German Jewish men, thousands of them
German Jewish men who had been captured in the net of Nazi frustration
Defeat at Stalingrad escalated the racial hate, the German Jewish men were targets
Slated for deportation, deportation to nowhere, to a place of no return

The Nazis wanted to murder those Jews, all Jews, but the laws they passed were complex
Under the 1935 Nuremberg laws, there were full Jews and other Jews
Jews married to Aryans, like children with mixed parentage, were termed *mischlinges*
Aryans married to German Jews were encouraged and threatened to divorce them
In the beginning of the Nazi regime, there were as many as 30,000 intermarried couples
Mostly, it was the German wives of German Jewish husbands who refused divorce
Their failure and refusal to divorce left German Jewish men on the streets of Berlin

On the streets of Berlin and other German cities, the yellow badges were an eyesore
Especially in Berlin, the Nazi power structure was insulted and infuriated
By the failure and refusal of the German wives to abandon their Jewish husbands
The round-up of those men began on February 27, 1943, and escalated
Hitler himself had ordered Nazi Party officials to undertake those actions ruthlessly
The officials received "carte blanche" authority to do as they needed to do
To arrest, detain and retain those Jews in a building on *Rosenstrasse*

There is an historical question, unresolved, as to whether the Nazi intent at that moment
Had been simply to make the streets of Berlin *judenfrie* (totally free of Jews)
Or if it had been undertaken with an imminent plan to deport them to the death camps
It should not matter, not matter at all, in judging the courage of their *Aryan* wives
At a time and in a place where civil disobedience had long been quelled and dispelled
Those wives, thousands of them, gathered to demand their husbands back
Peacefully, they marched and pleaded on *Rosenstrasse*, to get their husbands back

No one can overestimate the bravery and the courage which they displayed
To even start the protest; and then when threatened by SS men carrying guns
Machine guns with which the Nazi men could shoot and kill them all dead
They did not crack; they did not waver; instead additional wives and relatives
Joined the protest, and the Nazis chose not to shoot and kill, seeking to preserve the myth
Of total German loyalty and unity; the national and international press were watching

what was happening on Rosenstrasse; On March 6, 1943, the men were released
Temporarily, the Nazis said, but those husbands, almost all of them, survived the war.

March 28, 2019

One might speculate
That the *Rosenstrasse* wives were only acting selfishly
To save their husbands, their marriages, and their own lives
But any such speculation would be unworthy of the actual results

The news of the protests on *Rosenstrasse* had spread very quickly
Inside of Germany, by word of mouth, then internationally in news reports
Without knowing it, the *Rosenstrasse* women may have saved many other lives
Selflessly; In France alone, deportation of French Jews married to Gentiles
was also ceased and enjoined by the Nazis pending *Rosenstrasse*

They'd secretly avoided public disclosure and public discussion of the death camps
Of the factual actual intended fate of all of the deported Jews, German and others
They deemed the Final Solution to be akin to a major military secret
A critical component of their entire wartime strategy and undertakings

The Nazis feared public disclosure and public discussion of the facts
That their military undertakings included mass incineration of noncombatants
Cowards always fear public disclosure and public discussion of the actualities
The *Rosenstrasse* women's protest brought a little bit of light to those dark acts

Award Winner

They first found him in 1989
44 years after the war had ended
He had been invisible, undiscovered
Unknown to anyone; a person without an identity

Because, of course, he had multiple identities
Before the war, he was an Italian fascist fighter
He volunteered for the Army, fought in Ethiopia
Joined Franco's forces in the Spanish civil war

Received an official letter of thanks from General Franco
The letter gratefully included instructions
Instructions to Spanish agencies everywhere to aid him, if ever in need
If he was ever in need of Spanish diplomatic assistance

He never expected to be in need of Spanish diplomatic assistance
He was Italian, all Italian, from Padua
With many Italian Jewish friends, from Padua and also the Italian Army in Ethiopia
It is little known that many Italian Jews favored Mussolini, before the pact with Hitler

In 1942, Giorgio Perlasca was thirty-one years old
Finished with his Italian Army service, and anxious to stay out
He was most upset with Hitler's Third Reich, for many reasons
Politically, he considered himself neither fascist, nor socialist
He had witnessed inhumane massacres of civilians on both sides,
Had, himself, become mostly suspicious of the Germans, anti-Nazi

For business reasons he was based in Budapest,
When Hungarians were becoming more and more pro-German, pro-Nazi
Most definitely against the Jews, whether stateless or Hungarian
And those Jews, stateless and Hungarian, were desperately seeking letters of protection
Letters of protection from any neutral foreign embassies and consulates
Swedish, Spanish, Portuguese, Swiss, anywhere a Jew could go, to get out of there

Italy switched sides in 1943, when the King, Victor Emanuel
Chose, in opposition to Mussolini, to side with the Allies and against the Axis

In Budapest, the King's acts turned Giorgio Perlasca overnight into an enemy alien
As an enemy alien, even without any hostile acts, by him, he was arrested
Captured and imprisoned, held initially in a German POW camp
A German camp, near the Austrian border, from which he was released

Bravely, Giorgio Perlasca returned to Budapest, without any known agenda
But, using the secret letter of assistance the Franco government had given him
He received a Spanish passport and Spanish accreditation with a brand new name
Then and thereafter to be known as: Jorge Perlasca, a Spaniard
He also became an award winning actor with a single self-made role
He made himself out to be the new acting Spanish counsel in Budapest

It took incredible presumption, gumption and charm for Perlasca
To successfully pretend to have official status, as if permitted to act for Spain
He had a chance to do so, only because the Spanish consular office in Budapest
Was in total disarray, chaos prevailed, the existing officers deserted their posts
Perlasca had learned his way around the office when getting his own passport
Meanwhile, bombing and complex conflicts had become nightly events in Budapest

The Germans were losing to the Russians, yet even in the midst of their withdrawal,
Facing almost certain, predictable, German defeat and Nazi demise
The German Secret Service personnel and their Hungarian allies
Remained very busy in Budapest transporting more and more Jews to the death camps
Perlasca made himself just as busy, saving those Jews and interrupting
Those transports, running to railway stations, playing the role of Spanish superhero man

It bears restating now, that in 1944, in Budapest, the tension was extremely tight
Perlasca was Italian, not really Spanish, his own passport had been improperly issued
He was not a Spanish diplomat, or any kind of diplomat, not even a neutral person
Yet he teamed with real neutral diplomats, including Sweden's Wallenberg
Angelo Rotta of the Vatican and Friedrich Born of the International Red Cross
To get more than 5,000 Hungarian Jews papers which saved them from certain death

Giorgio Perlasca, an Italian, pretending to be Jorge Perlasca, Spanish, and a diplomat
Told the Germans, the SS, even Adolf Eichmann himself
That those Hungarians, and those stateless Jews were really Spanish citizens
Entitled to claim neutrality, to remain in Hungary, not be transported anywhere
Entitled to remain, he asserted, under the protections of the Government of Spain,
Perlasca's performance as a superhero was worthy of honor, reward and award.

don david Calderon y. Aroesty
November 18, 2017

An amazing man with an amazing history
Including his award-winning acting performance
Like many Holocaust heroes, he downplayed his role

"Wouldn't you?" he asked, "seeing Jewish children shot
for no good cause, wouldn't you have done the same?"
Since 1989, he has been honored in Israel and in Hungary
Giorgio Perlasca has been feted in Italy and in New York
But the award which sticks out and takes my breath away
Is the one he got from the King of Spain, for acting in the name of Spain
even while unauthorized by Spain, he was admitted to the Order of Isabella
With a pension for life, for his faithful service as a Spanish diplomat!

AWARD WINNER

Our Stars

In Europe during WWII, it was impossibly difficult to be a Jew
Jews were a target of humiliating hate and baiting
Forced to wear striped prison uniforms and yellow badges
Jews had no organized battalions, no meaningful weaponry
Fighting back was, for most all of us, never an option

Some resorted to evasion and escape
Hiding anywhere, under any rock
The odds were terrible, the consequences of capture worse
Against those odds, there were exceptions, few

So, it was amazing that in England, Australia
New Zealand, Canada, Hong Kong, India, and South Africa,
Throughout the entire UK, boys and men who knew the score
Were nonetheless enlisting in the cause, the cause against Nazi tyranny

Finally, America and the Americans entered into the fray
Human beings of every stripe and kind, mostly Christians
Took basic training, upped up and in again, preparing to face the monsters
In the greatest, saddest, most horrible killing, war, the world had ever known

It's never too late to tell them, how much we appreciate
The efforts, the battles won and lost, the ultimate sacrifices many made
They were our stars, all of them, bright lights in dismal times
Every single one of those soldiers and sailors, heroically answering the call

Some made it through to be recognized, and they certainly should have been
The greatest generation that ever was, every single one, and all of them
Most especially important to recognize the ones who didn't make it back
We can see the markers on former battlefields and at war memorials

We need to, certainly should, take all the time required
To honor the ones who remain among us, very few
And certainly of course to remember most decently the others
To say our prayers for the special stars, they were our stars

July 2016

Guiding Principles

It was 70 years after liberation
When Gene Klein, a survivor
A survivor of the camps, spoke up thoughtfully
"I have been thinking about it," he said
"Here's what I want you to remember,"
"After we are gone, when our memories must become yours,"

Must become yours "to avoid the mistakes of the past"
To avoid the mistakes of the past happening again
"Before the name-calling, the bricks thrown through windows"
"Long before the cattle cars were used to take us to the camps"
Our town in Hungary was charming, my father, a World War I veteran,
Who had fought for Hungary, my father owned a hardware store

We were not wealthy; we were secure like you, secure as Hungarians
In Hungary; our town was in the foothills of the beautiful Carpathian
Mountains; Life was good, ordinary, everyday life in the most basic of ways
But, all that ended earlier and then suddenly in the spring of 1944
My father's store was confiscated, taken away from him, from us
We teenagers were closed out of school, for the crime of being Jews

Forced to wear the yellow stars and driven from our homes
Soon, most Jews were taken to the camps, it was terrible, unbearable
The night closed out the daylight; SS officers in their black uniforms
Separated his father from him immediately upon arrival
He, a teenager, did not know why or where his father had gone
A veteran prisoner explained his father had disappeared in a wisp of smoke

The wonderful father he adored, as any teenage child would
He could, he should, harbor hate and great resentment about that
He was a witness against the SS barbarians who did those deeds
Not only the executioners, the SS librarians and other administrators too
The facilitators shouldn't be permitted to hide under their desks
Nor be able to plead "paper pushing" as a defense to murderous acts

He, himself, had a different experience which formed
Formed the basis for his guiding principles; Speaking German, as he did
he was assigned at camp to work for one German civil engineer, who saw

Saw the dreadful conditions and decided to help him, helped him
The engineer hid bits of food for him, every day, meat and cheese, rice and milk
By so doing, aimed to save his life, replenish his strength, renew his faith

It took a German in WWII to teach Gene Klein that no one should be judged
Solely based on nationality, race or religion; all humans can care for other humans
Surely, we are all capable of bad or good; we can all rise to amazing heights
Against all odds, the German engineer took an amazing risk, providing food to him
The German engineer escaped the Nazi propaganda which reduced Jews to subhumans
The German engineer saved his life, replenished his strength, renewed his faith

That is the lesson that Gene Klein shared with the world, importantly
All individuals must be judged by their own personal actions
We must never be swayed by sweeping allegations against "all of them"
We must constantly be vigilant against the descent from self-righteousness
To the dehumanization of others whose only offense is that they do not
Do not happen to share our skin color, national origin or religious beliefs

December 10, 2017

Gene Klein wrote the piece on which the "Guiding Principles" are based
Together with his daughter, Jill Klein, they together
Wrote a book about her father's Holocaust experience
We Got the Water: Tracing My Family's Path through Auschwitz
It takes a special strength, an almost incredible timber of character
To survive a great intentional fire of hate, and be able to shake
Your fist, only at the specific arsonists in that fire, and rationally
More meaningfully, alert future generations that we will all need
Knowledge and compassion, to avoid the mistakes of the past
Rightly warning us: It is too easy to engage in group hate
Too easy to engage in designations by race, religion, or nationality
Those are his Guiding Principles, learned from a German in WWII

Picture Perfect

Germany had gone through some terrible times, from 1914 to 1932
In World War I, it had kind of lost the war, without exactly being defeated
Not on the battlefield; It lost the will to fight, surrendered and sued for a peace treaty
Which turned out to be very much a one-way peace treaty, imposing and punitive
Established at Versailles, with taxes and tariffs, treating Germany badly
Limits and restrictions on what Germany could be, could do
And after the war was over, matters became worse, much worse
The German Mark had little value and Germans got little respect
The prices of things changed in Germany on a daily basis
Monday's bushel full of Marks for a barrel loaves of bread
Became Tuesday's barrel full of Marks for a bushel full of bread
Economic financial instability spread incessantly, Germany needed a new direction

That's when in 1933, in grave despair, Hitler gained control, and Nazism took over
A new system, a new Government, a new voice of stridency, urging self-confidence
Lots of wrongs were to be corrected, and Nazis promised militant acts to go with it
Militarism, troops and more troops, weapons and more weapons
The restrictions in the Versailles treaty were to be ignored or overturned
Plus, as a central focus of the Nazi era, damnation of its Jews, all Jews

There were a few, too few, within Germany who protested and protected
The German Jews, who quickly lost their rights, then their occupations
Their properties were taken from them as well, their world was crashing down
Those who could, would get out of there, if that was possible, soon not really possible
German Jews stuck in Germany were deemed to be, treated as, enemies of the State
Most of them had no rational reason for living there, and little, if any, chances of escape

In the 1930s, the Leica was a German engineered product, one to make them proud
A German camera, inventive, precise, minimalist, utterly totally efficient
Nazi armies used the Leica camera products, to be sure, they relied on them
They relied on Ernst Leitz II, the Protestant patriarch of the Leica companies
He headed up the firm, the family firm, it was his business to run, to run his way
In Germany and elsewhere, there were Leica stores in France, England and the USA

The senior Mr. Leitz operated his firm with uncommon grace, generosity and modesty
He was a good man, a Protestant Christian and a loyal German citizen, he found the way
He answered frantic calls from German Jewish employees and former associates
They had to, needed to, were required to, as a matter of life and death, to getaway

What could Leica do? What could Mr. Leitz do, consistent with his love for Germany?
Consistent with his love for Germany and his abiding respect for decency and humanity

He designed cover up stories to ship his German Jewish brethren to places faraway
To the Leica Camera stores all over the world, far and away from Germany
They traveled as Leica employees, sometimes as supposed employees, Mr. Lietz's guests
Headed, all of them were headed for Leica stores in far off foreign destinations
Employees, actually or not, truth be told, Jewish escapees on the Leica freedom train

don david Calderon y. Aroesty
2020

There is no regime, no matter how oppressive
Which cannot be worked around by some people
By the very courageous, very courageously
Willing to take extraordinary unselfish risks for others
Extraordinary risks to their own well being
Choosing to be exceptional, exceptionally

The Leitz family certainly loved Germany
But, first, above all else, they loved humanity
They are proofs that there are limits to patriotism
Limits which all true patriots will always observe
Doing the right thing for your country
First requires doing the right thing

VOLUME 2

A Matter of Honor

Defying his superiors in Tokyo, a principled man
Chiune Sugihara, the Japanese Vice-Consul
In Kovno, the second largest City in Lithuania, in 19 Hundred and 40
Issued transit visas to thousands of Jews seeking to escape Lithuania

They were seeking to escape from Lithuania just when the German Nazis
Were knocking on the door, preparing to invade, to walk into woe-begotten Lithuania
The exit transit visas the Japanese Vice-Consul provided permitted them to get away
To get away from one very cold nowhere to another very cold nowhere, Vladivostok

Vladivostok was the major Pacific Ocean port city in Russia
Near the terminus of the Trans-Siberian railway; there was nothing there, there
No reason at all to go to Vladivostok, excepting then the absence of German Nazis
And, ultimately, the only place in Russia, near Russia, with ocean access to Japan

No one would be waiting at the station or waving flags to welcome them in Vladivostok
Quite to the contrary, those thousands of Lithuanian Jews would be stranded there
For nine more months, until an additional Japanese man, a second man of honor,
Would and did undertake the task of escorting them, in small groups, the rest of the way

Tatsuo Osaka, a tourist bureau clerk, nothing more than that, an ordinary clerk
No official title, no diplomatic privilege, no grant of authority from Japan or any agency
He undertook to escort many of those bedraggled folks in small and separate groups
On ferry trips from Vladivostok to Japan, in 1940 and 1941, before Pearl Harbor happened

The Japanese were not yet at war with the Western world, but even after December 7th
When the world turned upside-down, the furious conflicts extended to the Pacific
The Lithuanian Jews who had been saved were still saved, and were never surrendered
Japan never surrendered them to the Germans and the fires of the Holocaust.

February 12, 2019

Don't ever let anyone ever tell you they know the secret
As to who, how and why some people act with extreme bravery and honor
When the great majority are being swayed to go along, to get along
With acts we all will later know and understand to have been dishonorable

Interestingly, it seems to be, that it is usually the untitled or lesser titled ones
Vice-Consuls, Tourist Bureau Clerks, ordinary citizens without privileges
The ones who have no special stripes or unique identifying characteristics
It is a puzzle; the whole of the puzzle is puzzling: honor is highly unpredictable

In combination with bravery, honor must be provided by a very recessive gene,
Only the few seem to come forward, muster the character to do the unexpected
They do amazing things honorably, often without any known Earthly reward

Cousin Rachel

Albania was a dark and mysterious
Place, more communistic than communism
And Moslem, a majority Moslem state
The only majority Moslem nation
In all of Europe; the Nazis expected
Expected the Albanians to be anti-Jewish
After all, they thought, the Koran is anti-Jews
Mohammed is quoted saying bigoted things

It did not turn out that way
In that place, Albania, there was hardly a trace
Of bigotry, racial or religious discrimination
In the 1930s and the 1940s
This small, complex, mountainous country
In the southwest corner of the Balkans
Right next door to Macedonia and Monastir
Was a real rarity, without religious hate

In Albania, officially, hate did not exist
Was not allowed to perpetuate
They protected their Jewish citizens
Plus, they provided safe harbor to Jewish refugees
They observed the code of Besa, kept the promise
The promise to protect traveling strangers
Best as one could/should protect one's own family

The Albanians did us a special favor
They held out their hands, extended their peaceful arms
While the Jews of Macedonia, including Monastir
Were to be and being transported to Treblinka
For final resolution, Albanians arranged a different solution
For one of ours, one of our own, they saved Cousin Rachel

don david Calderon y. Aroesty
October 15, 2017

On October 7, 2017, in Wayland, Massachusetts
Cousin Rachel celebrated her 100th birthday
In the presence of other cousins, Americans
Italians, Swiss and Israeli, many descending
From Monastir in Macedonia, proudly
Remembering the common heritage, the invisible ties
Properly crediting Macedonia and the Macedonians
For many things over many, many years, before
Before the Nazi tragedies and Holocaust
Also applauding Albania and the Albanians
Whoever saves the life of one innocent stranger
Mercifully, saves the promise of justice and decency
For the entire world to see; and emulate. Amen.

Albania—Chapter 2

Payback, the least we could do
On November 26, 2019
An all-powerful earthquake
Arrived uninvited and unwanted in Albania
Fifty-five people were instantaneously killed
Thousands were injured
Many more thousands were rendered homeless

The blast was horrendous, 6.4 magnitude on the Richter scale
Israel promptly sent a cadre of military and civilian engineers
To help all of Albania, right after the quake, to help all of Albania
Determine which buildings were safe and which were not occupiable
The President of Albania realized and recognized the Israeli assistance
He thanked the President of Israel sincerely, Muslim to Jew, they knew

They, the both of them, knew the history which escapes too many other eyes
Albania was the only country, the only country under occupation in WWII
Where there were more Jews alive and living after the war than before
Before the Holocaust had swept like a plague through all of Europe
The numbers in Albania were very small, perhaps mathematically meaningless
The principle was/is memorable; we have a duty to remember and never to forget

A group, a small group of Israeli Jews, an organization called From the Depths
Remembered, and they undertook to travel to Albania, on their own
They also went right after the quake, intending to help in any way they could
Albanians had offered food and shelter to the Jews when food and shelter was absent
The Albanian King, King Zog I, had issued 2,000 visas to stranger Jews
Allowing them, permitting them, to pass through, to safely inhabit Albania

In 1996, *Yad Vashem*, in Israel, had recognized the family of Muhamet Bicaku
A Muslim man from Albania whose father and brother had rescued
Rescued twenty Jewish families from Nazi occupation forces in Albania
They, the Bicakus, stand among the righteous of the world for what they did
When we were on our backs, unable to help ourselves without the help of others
From the Depths invests in payback, doing whatever we can do, when we can do

In 2019, they rebuilt the home of Muhamet Bicaku in the wake of that awful quake
It was payback, the very least we ought do, as Jews, to help others who helped us
During the most difficult and trying of times, when help was almost impossible

Invisible

He was born in the town of Wegrow
In northeastern Poland, in 1938
Not a propitious time and place
For any child to be born, especially a Jew

The Nazi Army was later crossing Poland
Knocking down the obstacles *en route* to Russia
Soldiers, trucks, tanks, supplies and more
Crossing Poland at its northeastern sector

Opening an eastern front, the Nazis were joyous
Having smashed and humiliated many other nations
The Germans were singing and swaying, almost dancing
With a confident sense of jubilation about the conflict

About the conflict, yet to begin, in earnest, with the Russians
He remembers this: his father did not even know
His father did not even know for whom to root
The Germans were viscous, unforgivably, but the Russians often
Seemed mindless, carbon copies of the hate, which reigned in the region

His father had a strategy for his family: it was invisibility
Invisibility and hoping for a stalemate, which kept both protagonists
Busy with each other, until eternity, and meanwhile he would build
He would not build structures, not at all, nothing visible
He intended to build underground bunkers, places to hide, to live and hide

Live and hide, in order to survive, in order to survive invisibly
He would build the first such bunker on his own farm property
Under an existing wooden storage shed behind the house
An ingenious scheme, he dreamed of it, then wished for it, prayed for it
And as the beginning of the Nazi-Russian conflict raged, he implemented it

Eventually, even though stymied by the Russians at Stalingrad
The Nazis and their henchmen, they had plenty of henchmen
Returned to pay attention to the Polish Jews, intending to send them all away
Away, not for a vacation, a simple *spotshir*, two days in the sun or at the beach
No, they intended instead to make the Jews disappear permanently, a final solution

Eddie Bielawski's father outmaneuvered the Nazis, the bunker worked
Hidden beneath the earth, covered with plywood boards, soil and straw
Made indistinguishable from the rest of the earthen floor
A trap door to get them in and out, occasionally, while
Air and water flowed through separate sets of drainage pipes

They weren't the only Poles who hid and lived invisibly
Others were hidden by friendly neighbors; some moved to the other side
Seeking to make believe they were Polish Catholic Christians
Very few Jewish families fully avoided and evaded the terrible conditions
That's the horrific truth of it, invisibility was but a minor tactic, gimmickry
Saving a fortunate few fortuitously, whilst the vast majority fell victim to the storm

don david Calderon y. Aroesty
December 5, 2018

Based on an excerpt from "Invisible Jews"
Surviving the Holocaust in Poland, by Eddie Bielawski
Except as a temporary tactic, one cannot hide from injustice
You must arise, whenever possible, to fully challenge the devils

Mister President

He always was a good old boy, a native son of the South
Before he was the majority leader of the US Senate
He always was a good old boy, of that there was little doubt
Before he inherited the Presidency, most unexpectedly
And then, the question arose, would he champion the civil rights fight
Of course he would, he had a history practically no one knew or fully understood

He was from a Texan political family which was full of spit and vinegar
Decency and fair play was in his blood, taught to him from when he wore knee-highs
Southerners, they were against the KKK and other groups of violent hate and bigotry
And so it was when he was grown and on his own, he did not have to wait and see He judged Mr. Hitler
    on his very own words, Nazism was another instrument of hate No one needed to convince LBJ that
    intervention would be necessary and correct
When the Holocaust of hate and misery commenced in Europe,
He was one of the early observers who observed that the Jews needed to get out of there
In Texas, in America, thousands of miles away from it, he did what he could
As a Congressman, he arranged for visas to be supplied to some Jews in Warsaw
A few, not a lot, they, at least, could getaway, avoid, evade the catastrophe to happen
Closer to home, he also lent a hand, to hundreds of Jews entering the US via Galveston

No one knew or would have expected that of him, he was always such a good old boy
Underneath that southern skin, as it happened, there was a mighty righteous gentile soul
As he proved once again after Kennedy's assassination, when he served as the shepherd
For the entire flock of us, ushering in the passage of the full civil rights legislation
Who knew? Who would have expected it of him? Erich Leinsdorf was one
That musician and conductor, Jew, his life was saved by LBJ before WWII.

don david Calderon y. Aroesty
2020

Erich Leinsdorf's musical credentials are overwhelming
He was a child prodigy in Austria before WWII
In 1937, Erich had come to America to serve
As an assistant conductor at the Met in NY
Then, when the *Anschluss* happened and
Austria became part of Nazi Germany
He was threatened with being shipped back to Austria
If he had been shipped back to Austria, he likely would have been dead

But a freshman Congressman from Texas, LBJ, arranged
For Erich Leinsdorf to become a US Citizen, amen
He who saves one innocent life saves the entirety of civilization
LBJ's later record with respect to the US Involvements
In Vietnam, may cause others to scratch and wonder
This vignette is neither an endorsement nor a critique generally
It is about LBJ's perceptiveness re: the Holocaust and his willingness to act

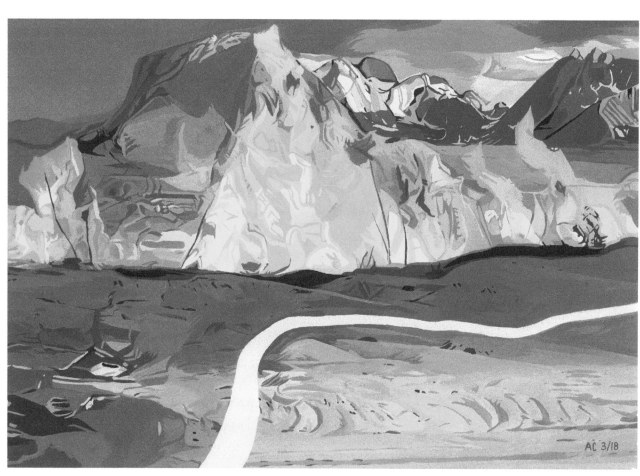

GUIDING PRINCIPLES/CAPARTHIAN MOUNTAINS

Greedy, Selfish, Bastard

There were, there are, far too few stories like this one
When, many decades after the happening of the Holocaust, we are told of some hero
Previously unreported, it is met no doubt, with great doubt, questions
As to reliability, credibility, sources and documentation, that's why when one
When one backed by undeniable documents, facts and figures, names and faces
The disclosure ought warm the cockles of our hearts: it's real, he's real.

Many people knew him or claimed to know of him
Some of them, if they could, would describe him in few words
Especially apt words: "greedy, selfish, bastard" ill-tempered and ruthless too
Not that they really knew, they didn't know, and that's the point of this

Mauricio (Moritz) Hochschild
It rhymes with Rothschild, and that's where the similarity ends, we're told
He was best known as a swashbuckling Bolivian tin tycoon, when Bolivia,
The whole entire country, was like an under supervised wild western town

He had been born in Germany, a German Jew,
In Europe, when the fuss after WWI was just beginning, he got out of there
He made his way, all the way, circa 19 hundred and 20, from a mining family
To Bolivia, to Tin, to untold riches, to almost uncountable sums

He was short in stature, long on accomplishments, a focused doer
He had a Hitler mustache, it looked almost cartoonish
Quickly became one of the three Bolivian "Tin Barons"
They, the three of them, controlled all Tin mining in Bolivia

Just when the metal was needed more and more by the whole industrial world
Arising from a deep depression, reviving everywhere
Tin brought many foreign customers and much foreign currency
To Bolivia, winning Mauricio entree and influence,
including with Bolivia's military President, German Busch

That's when his abysmal reputation first developed
They called him callous, unprincipled
A widower early in life, he had an affair with a cousin's wife, later married her
The rumors spread, he cared only about himself, the crowd presumed to know
He was long reviled, actual memories slipped and were forgotten

It took until 2017 to correct the record
In 2017, the Mining Corporation of Bolivia
A conglomeration of the old tin baron properties
They had nationalized Hochschild's tin mines in 1952

Sixty-five years later, they accidentally found a treasure trove
Of very old documents, filthy, ragged, garbage
The papers were in terrible condition, they might have been discarded, thrown away
They were not, it took fortitude and diligence multiplied by curiosity to continue

The documents revealed that Mauricio Hochschild
Far from being only self-concerned, had tried to save the world from Fascism
First, he tried to sponsor political opposition to that contagious disease, and when
that failed, he set his sights pointedly on saving Jews stuck in Europe

He used his connections in Bolivia, including with the President
To secure foreign visas for European Jews
He personally stimulated, orchestrated and made sure it worked
That there would be an Express *Judio* from various points to La Paz, Bolivia

He enabled them to leave both by ship or smaller boats
Headed first to Latin America, any port would do, then to La Paz
Once safely in Bolivia, he would undertake to arrange for them
To be able to find jobs, housing, schools and local aid

He underestimated the scope of the problems to get that done
Almost every one of them spoke not a single word of Spanish
Many were penniless as well; so he started, founded and funded
Two social organizations to protect and help the new immigrants

From 1938, when he started, to mid-1939
9,000 to 12,000 Jews left Europe for La Paz, successfully
Even if it was 12,000 Jews, a pitiful handful compared to the 6,000,000
Hochschild saved more Jewish souls in those years than the whole of most countries

Best as the record reveals, never seeking reward for himself,
Not money, not applause, nothing selfish at all he gave credit to Bolivia and Bolivians
For taking the Jewish immigrants in, there was hostility in other places
Learning this in 2017, the Mining Corporation of Bolivia
has treated Hochschild, long deceased, almost as a national hero

Who the hell was he anyway, this little man
Still wearing then his prominent Hitler mustache
While the world stood still, did not do enough, not nearly enough
To stop the Holocaust or at least confront the fact that it was occurring

Don't blame Mauricio Hochschild, he did his share, more than his share
He bet his life on it, no greedy, selfish bastard was he.

don david Calderon y. Aroesty
October 05, 2020

German Busch, thirty-five and president, declared himself dictator for life, April 23, 1939; his first order was the execution of Hochschild, but Busch failed—August/39 was a suicide.

Mr. Doctor

He was not exactly Jewish, he was most certainly not, not Jewish
Religiously, he would have described himself as agnostic
But he believed, he did, he believed in children's rights
He was a prolific writer and proponent for children's causes

Perhaps, you never heard of him; you should and ought look him up
Born Henryk Goldszmit, he grew up to be a Polish doctor-educator
He adopted the pen name of Janusz Korczak, and under that pen name
He wrote many children's books, served as director of a Warsaw orphanage

He was educated initially as a pediatrician
Worked at children's hospitals, first used his pen name in 1898
While still a student, an observer of human behavior and a children's advocate
Served as a military doctor during the Russo-Japanese war, and again in WWI

After the great war, he had his own Polish, Polish-language, radio program
On which Doctor Janusz first promoted and popularized children's rights and adult
Responsibilities; he became well-known and highly respected throughout Poland
He was awarded the Silver Cross of the Polish Restituta

When the Germans invaded in 1939, he volunteered again for the Polish Army
He was turned down, rejected, by reasons of age, returned to the role of orphanage
Administrator, of a Jewish children's orphanage, though offered repeatedly
Sanctuary on the other side, by the Polish underground, he declined, "No, thank you"

He wanted, he said repeatedly, to stay with his children, not to abandon them
Inevitably, the inevitable happened in 1942, the SS cleaned out the orphanage
Took all of the children, mostly tots of only two and three, some older, teens, perhaps
The oldest resident was said to be thirteen; Dr. Janusz Korczak voluntarily went along

He had them dress, neatly and cleanly, for the trip to the central railroad station
And from there, straight to Treblinka for the final solution; there was no heroic outcome
The end of the line was the end of the line for Dr. Janusz Korczak and all of his Warsaw
Orphans; he had spent a lifetime issuing careful warnings against child abuse
Those careful warnings were burned with him and with his orphans as well in Treblinka

don david Calderon y. Aroesty
May 9, 2018

In Warsaw, there is an important monument to Korczak

It shows him sadly, but proudly, standing erect, leading all his children to the trains

He is remembered fondly in all of Poland, a heroic and correct doctor-father figure

He was Mr. Rogers, before there was a Mr. Rogers in the USA or anywhere

He published over 1400 children-centric texts in around 100 publications

About 300 of his texts are in manuscript (book-length) form

Including King Matt the First and Kaytak the Wizard (translated to English)

Words alone can never surmount the pain; words alone provide only glimpses

Bittersweet memories, were it only possible to prescribe a certain path to safety

Something to Talk About

The Nazi policies of genocide
Of the entirety of European Jewry
Followed a pattern which repeated
In almost every occupied country

Identification and dehumanization
Restrictions on livelihood and living conditions
Confiscation and appropriation
Segregation from the non-Jewish population

The disappearance of
"They" "Them," "The rats and vermin"
Is so much easier to explain than your
Neighbors, friends, family doctor,
Shopkeeper, teacher, student, grandmotherly
Nannies too, and all of them were to be
Crammed into train transports; stored like refuse
In refuse heaps, on route to foreign camps

Mass liquidations carried out secretly
Without publicizing the accumulating smoking clouds and
Aggregate counts of innocent victims from the insanity of genocide
Though it was surely no secret strategy, making Europe
Judenrein (rid of Jews) was the key word
The capital cause and course for Nazism
And the civilized world surely knew of it
They needed no more photos of the camps

In the midst of those unspeakable horrors
The miracle of the Danish Jews in Denmark
Is a story of survival and exceptionalism
Exceptional Jews and exceptional Danes

National character and principled behavior
Trees which bend and do not break
Their unselfish bravery in crisis conditions requires
Telling and retelling many, many times

The community in Denmark
Had existed since the 17th Century
Initially, they were Portuguese merchants
Transplants from the Iberian expulsions

Supplemented over time by other waves of immigrants
Principally piously committed to our ancient faith
Gratefully loyal to the host Danish Christian Kings
Danish artfully became their valued mother tongue

For 300 years, Jews had lived in Copenhagen and every nook and cranny
Of Denmark; they had been farmers and fishermen, husbands and fathers
Scholars and businessmen; They had prayed to God and counted on the King
Over the years, they experienced evolving political emancipation
And economic opportunities, side by side with other Danes
Denmark was uniquely free of ghettos and ghettoized thinking

In 1940, the Germans invaded on April 9
Denmark surrendered within hours, choosing not to fight a losing battle
The King and civil authorities entered instead into a cooperation agreement
On condition that Denmark retain its King, Parliament and sovereignty
Including, critically, exclusive dominion over its Danish Jewish population
Ceding, in the process, to the Germans, control over stateless Jews

From April, 1940 to the fall of 1943
Three and a half years of history's most frightful events elsewhere
While the Danes were militarily cooperating with the Germans
Even against the Russians, the Germans left the Danish Jews alone

They remained in their Danish Jewish homes, and integrated neighborhoods
Remained in their private and public professions and occupations
King Christian X retained his Danish Jewish Doctor; it was or
Seemed to be, normalcy while the rest of Europe burned insidiously

The Danish Jews even retained their synagogues
Where they stayed and prayed, untouched by German hands
Despite the Danish cooperation, the Jews doubtlessly seeking the Almighty's
Intervention, prayed again against these evil pharaohs of the modern age

In the end, like Moses, the Danish resistance awoke and rose up against the Nazis
Spiking in August of 1943 and the German armies there reacted forcefully
Deciding on the 29th to permanently impose German military control in Denmark
The Danish Government and Parliament immediately resigned
The King was put under house arrest; it was, they feared
The beginning of the end for the Danish Jews
The Germans had planned a general roundup of the Danish Jews
Telling no one the date, it was scheduled for October 1, 1943

Danish authorities continued to intervene and to plead for their Jews
Arguing, in the interim, seemingly successfully, for German moderation
Such moderation and a leaked early warning to the Danes and the Jews
Permitted the Danes and the Jews to implement a mosaic miracle

An almost total escape of the Danish Jewish population across the risky straits
Hidden in fishing boats, they were transported from Denmark to nearby neutral Sweden
As a result of which, about 99 percent of the Danish Jews survived the war, the entire war
To the great credit of Denmark and the Danes, their Jews survived the Nazi Holocaust

Copenhagen, October 1, 2017

**With thanks and full credit to Sofie Lene Bak, author and compiler
Of "Nothing to Speak Of"—Wartime Experiences of the Danish Jews
And Bjarke Folner, Museum Curator of the Danish Jewish Museum
Their exceptional presentation of the Danish experience is at once
Scholarly and enthralling; eye-opening on many levels
Unfortunately, the world once again needs eye-opening observations.**

Leaves Quietly Applauding

On this day
Like many other days
In the region of Normandy
Close to the *cote Atlantique*
On this day, like many other days
The sun is angled down, shining brightly
Above, the thin and narrow clouds quickly pass
Picturesquely, as if on an artist's palette
The wind, this day, is gently swirling
Leaves on the branches of the tallest
Of the towering trees, seem to me to be
Quietly applauding, perhaps remembering
Those of every nation and national grouping
Who've fallen here, were buried here

We traipse through the countryside
Though not unaware, neither are we
Consciously recalling, that these *quaint villes*
Kilometres removed from the cemeteries on the beaches
Were, here too, modern history teaches, also imprinted
With the blood of *les etrangers*
Foreign troops fighting foreign troops, each side dying
Each side dying so that, when it was finished, the flags
Of liberty, equality and fraternity would, once again, wave
Wave, just like the leaves quietly applauding

No one side has a monopoly on right
Sometimes, it is indistinguishable from
Wrong, dressed as screaming grievances
Please, God, forever forbid
A one to one relationship
Between the victims and the victimizers
Though both may have struggled
Fought furiously, famously, some even valiantly
In the end, there will always be an end
The candles must be lit, most piously
For those who strove, most earnestly
Seeking to bring about the light

From the darkness, which ruled in its absence
The troops of the United States, the United Kingdom,
Including Canada, and the free French forces, all together
Established a beachhead in western Europe in June of 1944
It was the beginning of the end of the darkest days and nights
The world had ever known, and the known world had ever experienced

Normandy, France, July 2016

Visiting, learning, remembering; reliving the lessons of yesteryear
Holding our collective breath that it will never be necessary again
Never be necessary again, to mobilize millions of men
To meet and defeat monsters, dripping blood from their teeth

The Holocaust before and during World War II
Did not just end, out of its obese desperation
First, an entire continent was infected and infested
With blind mindlessness, resulting in systematic frenzied violent excesses

Each destroyed community of Jews was never enough
To quell the appetite of the death machine and its machinists
Even as the Axis armies were floundering, the Nazi Jew-killers
Remained at large, at their stations while beginning their escape

D-Day was the beginning of the end of the conflict known as WWII
The Brits, the Canadians, the Free French, and mostly, the Yanks
They, bravely united, stormed the beaches, into the cyclonic whirlwinds of war
At last, at last, thousands of men, good and true, were standing up

Standing up to the Axis; Allies, joined by the Russians, advancing from the east,
Were prepared to take back an entire continent gone to hell
It would be another nearly full year, twelve more months
Before, finally, the Nazi war operations surrendered and ceased

And the disastrous death camps were fully discovered, and uncovered
Our remembrances would surely be insufficient and totally lacking
If the greatest generation, those allied troops, both the many who made the ultimate
Sacrifice, and the fortuitous survivors, our fathers, elder brothers, uncles and
Neighbors, if they or any of them, were omitted from the list of Holocaust heroes

May they, heroes and heroines, never be forgotten or less than fully appreciated
They did not start the conflict or the Holocaust; they did not permit it
They, all of them, who fought against the Nazis, brought an end to the genocide
When, as and in the only way possible, by defeating the Nazis in the battlefield
Their courage, their bravery, must always be quietly correctly applauded

GREATEST GYMNAST EVER (VERSION ONE)

The Greatest Gymnast Ever

The 1956 summer Olympics took place in Melbourne, Australia
While the events were ongoing in Melbourne, Australia
And their Olympic athletes respectively were competing respectfully with one another
Russian tanks and troops invaded Hungary, cutting off any chance of Hungarian freedom
Behind the Iron Curtain, the Russians enforced the Iron Curtain, suffocating that chance

The invasion also ruined any possible, and suitable, Hungarian Olympiad celebration
Which, might, otherwise have taken place; because, simultaneously, a Hungarian lady
Who was 35 years old, 35 years old, a gymnast, that's almost, in gymnastics,
A senior citizen person, she had won gold medals in three individual floor events
Three gold medals out of four individual floor events, an almost unbelievable feat,
And that's but a fraction, a tiny fraction, of her absolutely amazing life story

She was born Agnes Klein in Hungary, in 1921
She was a gymnast from early youth, started competing when she was 4 years old
She became the Hungarian National Champion in 1937, 1937; she was then 16 years old
She also was National Champion 9 more times later, after 1937 and before 1956
Still, a tiny fraction of her absolutely amazing life story; you have to pay attention now

She was a Jew, a Hungarian Jew, in her early years there were many well-known Jews
Successful in many professions, learned, achievement-minded, others stand up and stand out
Proud to be both Hungarian and Jewish; they played the Hungarian national anthem
When Agnes won in Melbourne and she stood at attention on the podium as they played
In 1956, but in between, after '37, there had been a long dark, very dark, period

The Kingdom of Hungary was a member of the Axis nations affiliated with the Nazis
Not merely affiliated, they took their own forceful steps both at home and abroad
Make no excuses for them, when the greatest challenge in the history of the world, so far
Was happening, the Hungarians chose to be, chose to be, on the wrong side of it

Surely, they wanted to get out from under the depression, all nations wanted to overcome
That worldwide disastrous decline; everyone had been spinning in the down direction
Some thought it possible to climb out of the condition simply by blaming the Jews
While other nations understood that recovery required unity, strength by sticking together
Hungary and the Hungarians, for whatever reason, chose the wrong side of that equation

Hungary did not merely side with Germany; it actively participated in WWII
It wanted land from the Czech Republic, land from Slovakia, more territory
It also wanted to make sure that it out-Nazi'd its archrival, Romania
Hungarian troops fiercely fought with the German panzer divisions in Russia
They had some small victories, but in the end, they were crushed by the Russians

Hungary also actively participated in the Holocaust; sometimes it appeared as if
The Government in Hungary was modifying, moderating, changing every other week;
Sometimes more liberal, sometimes less tolerant; eventually, there was no doubt about it
While the exact numbers are much in dispute, starting in 1944, many, many thousands
Perhaps as many as 800,000 Hungarian Jews died in the concentration camps
Maybe, one out of every three persons incinerated at Auschwitz had been Hungarian

During the war, Agnes avoided being shipped to the camps by being fleet afoot
First, she married, in a marriage likely of "necessary convenience," a Christian gymnast
Costar, Istvan Sarkany; then by purchasing and using false Christian ID papers
Finally, by working as a maid, in a small remote village; hiding her mother and sister
Ultimately, getting their papers from the famous Swedish diplomat, Raoul Wallenberg

Agnes's father did not escape; he was among those who died in Auschwitz
Still she had the temerity to remain in Hungary and return to Hungarian gymnastics
Right after the war, she resumed her career in gymnastics, successfully
She was national champion again; she qualified for the 1948 Olympics, but
did not participate, due to an injury, which would have permanently sidelined others

Not Agnes Sarkany, nee Klein; instead, she resumed training, and competed strongly
In the 1952, Helsinki, Finland Olympics, when she was already thirty-one years old
She earned four medals, one gold, one silver, two bronze, gratifying, terrific
That would have been amazing enough for most; Agnes continued her endeavors.

In 1956, she added six more medals, three gold, for a total of four, ten medals in all
The Hungarian gymnastics team carried on her back finished second in the whole world
Their silver medal even outshining the Russians whose Army at the same time squashed
and occupied their homeland, so much so, that she and 44 other Hungarian athletes
Refused to return to Hungary and decided instead to seek and obtain political asylum

Asylum in Australia was a stopover for Agnes Klein Keleti; she found her new true home
She emigrated to Israel in 1957; she's lived In Israel now for more than sixty years
The majority of her time she's been an Israeli physical education instructor
At Tel Aviv University and Wingate Sports Institute in Netanya; no fading rose is she
She also coached and worked with the Israeli national gymnastics team well into her 90s

She is in the Hungarian Sports Hall of Fame
In the International Jewish Sports Hall of Fame
She remains the oldest female gymnast ever to win Olympic gold
They didn't give any prizes for dealing with the Holocaust

If they did, she would surely win, she did a triple double jump from the trapeze of death
To the invisible, only barely imaginable, floor, bars and balance beams of real life
She survived and became a champion again; she led Hungary to Olympic gold
And, then, flew home, safely and securely, to Israel, for gold again in her golden years
In 2017, at age ninety-six, she was announced laureate of the Israeli prize in sports.

April 6, 2017

If this were fiction, no one could write it believably
It is true, factual, Agnes Klein Keleti was Superwoman
Before that character was invented, and not only for her skills at gymnastics
She endured during the Holocaust, never in a camp, never physically imprisoned
She nonetheless felt the enormous weight of the enmity, the murder of her father,
The fatal disappearance of so many thousands of her fellow Hungarian Jews

She never let those things destroy her faith, or her belief in the capacity of mankind
When she competed, she trained to succeed, she expected to succeed
When she successfully emigrated to Israel, she immediately sent for her family
She was with her mother and her sister
She is with her whole entire greater Israeli family

It is a mystery without answers why she choose to compete for Hungary
To compete for Hungary when she knew its leaders had been complicit
Complicit during WWII in the Holocaust and the murder of her father
The murder of her father and many thousands of other Hungarian Jews

The history of Agnes Klein may be a mystery which baffles some scholars
And the rest of us; there is no specific answer, no simple explanation,
Except, perhaps, the obvious ones about all of us, Jews in a gentile world
Historically, Jews seek to fit in, to belong and to be creative and productive
We seem to share, genetically, internal drives both to excel and to get along,
It is existential and gratifying, to be loyal and true members of a national team,
We reach out, and outreach, to be both Jew, and among the best in the universe

The Righteous

There were many, many stories
There were more than a million stories too few
The ones that happened and can be documented are unforgettable
They must be remembered and retold; it is like a commandment

A little girl, not twelve years old, she lived in a small village outside of Warsaw
A friendly village, one not yet totally infected with virulent anti-Semitism
Some people were kind, definitely Anti-Nazi; they did not want the Germans there
The Poles formed themselves into resistance units, part of a minor resistance army

The German Nazis succeeded in only days, they bombed and strafed and
Its land forces met with little opposition; soon they had overrun all of Poland
For the Jews of that godforsaken land, there were no easy remedies for the dilemma
The choices seemed to be between surrender and compliance, or hiding and escape

Who would hide a Jew? Who would possibly take the risk facing penalties of death
Or worse than death, having your whole family slaughtered before your very own eyes
It would take a special righteousness, strength of character made with spines of steel
Plus, a gambler's mentality, the willingness to undertake risks too risky to contemplate

Still, there were some, some very exceptional ones, who actually stepped forward
And hid the Jews; Henia Rozen, the twelve-year-old girl, her entire family was protected
Sheltered, housed and hidden by the Olbryskas, neighbors, not more, unselfishly
Charitably, they were Christians who understood the meaning of their Christianity

There was another family, Strzelecka, who joined in the effort, magnificently
They took Henia into their home, specifically, as if she was another daughter
A member of the family, to take to church and school with them, hand in hand
With their other children, until the war did finally end for Henia and her family
Her surviving family, lucky exceptions they were, could finally leave and go to Israel

For those heroes such as the Olbryskas and Strzleckas, thank you, a million thank you
messages would not be enough, a statue honoring such courageous acts also insufficient
In *Yad Vashem*, Israel, they have a garden to house the flowered tributes to the righteous
The world, it seems, will not fully learn and understand the ultimate price of bigotry
Hate knows no limitations; to meet and defeat it, righteousness is required mutually
For all of us to rest at ease on earth and triumph ultimately in salvation.

don david Calderon y. Aroesty
April 3, 2017

There is a recognized and well-respected charity
The Jewish Foundation for the Righteous
For the righteous of every other religion and nationality
Who risked their necks and their entire lives
When the world needed miraculous acts by heroes and heroines,
The world especially needed really righteous unselfishness

Amazing Grace

When she died in 2011, her ashes were sprinkled in an area of France
which had been the site of one of the French Resistance's major victories

She was Nancy Grace Augusta Wake, and if you've never heard of her
You should, she is one of WWII's most decorated civilians
She holds honors and titles from Australia, New Zealand, France, the US
And mostly from the UK; She was an amazing heroine throughout the conflict

She had been born in Wellington, New Zealand in 1912
The youngest of six children in a simple working class family of modest means
She could trace her ancestry to one Great Grandmother, a native Maori
One of the first to intermarry with a European, who'd come to New Zealand

Her family moved to Australia, North Sydney, when she was only two
It did not work for her father, he returned to New Zealand, leaving her mother
In Australia with the six children, Nancy Grace's growing up years were limited
At age 16, before completion of preparatory school, she herself ran away

Initially, she lived in London and worked as a nurse or a nurse's aide
In the 1930s, with linguistic skills, she became a newspaper foreign correspondent
She traveled in Europe, she witnessed the rise of Hitler and Nazism
She was in Vienna when roving gangs of Nazis were terrorizing Jews

She became emotionally committed to the fight against the Nazis, before
Before there was a war, she knew it was coming, and was internally prepared
In 1937, she was 25, and married well in France, to Henri Fiocca, an industrialist
They were living in Marseilles, along the French Riviera, a socialite's existence

In 1940, the Germans invaded France, and France soon surrendered
The north and Atlantic west came under direct German control
The southern part connected to the Mediterranean became Vichy France
Technically, still France, but committed to collaboration with the Nazis

Nancy Grace Augusta Wake Fiocca had no intention of collaborating with the Nazis
She almost immediately became a courier for the French resistance
And, slowly, she and her husband became more and more enmeshed with the resistance
With the efforts to fight the Nazis, and with the plight of refugees seeking to escape

In France, this seeming socialite who, of course, had been no child of privilege
Actively and energetically did everything she could to stifle and defeat the Nazis
Anonymously, she was the Gestapo's number 1 enemy, they called her the white mouse
Because she had eluded and deluded them so often, they established a 5-Million Franc
5-Million Franc reward offer for her, and someone betrayed the white mouse

Furnished with her name and identity, the Nazis were closing in on her
In 1943, she herself had to escape, had to flee France, and she did so
She made it across the Pyrenees, to Spain and then back to London
aided by her husband's refusal, after capture, to talk and give up her whereabouts
Henri Fiocca had been tortured, tormented, beaten and brutally killed by the Gestapo

Back in London, Nancy Grace Augusta Wake Fiocca also was not giving up
She volunteered to be of assistance, any assistance; the allies might require
The allies did require her assistance, D-Day was coming, they knew that secret
On March 1, 1944, despite the awful risks to her life and safety, they sent her back

To be a spy, she parachuted back into the center of German occupied France
She joined up with the Marquisyards, she became one of them in that critical moment
The Marquisyards were likely the most successful of all the French resistance units
Of all the French resistance units, they had accounted for 70 percent of the German casualties
While the Marquisyards had likely incurred only 1 percent of the French resistance losses

Nancy Grace helped to deter and keep the Germans occupied when D-Day was coming
After the war was over, she remarried and led a full additional life,
She received accolades, awards and many honors in recognition
Of her special efforts, which were truly special, something unique, entirely different

She'd served as a courier, a warrior, and as a spy; She'd excelled in all her roles
Once, she'd killed a German sentry, who needed to be killed—with a single karate chop
She could and did soberly out-think and out-drink her liquor laden enemies to get secrets
She, at times, demeaned her own successes, calling herself, "a flirtatious little bastard"

There is no way, no good and proper way, to sufficiently say enough about this heroine
Whether it was her simple background, or her Maori ancestry, whatever motivated her
We do not know; never quite French, though married for eternal love to a Frenchman,
who'd sacrificed his life for his wife to enable her to carry on the cause for France
In perfect French pronunciation, she declared all the causes and reasons for total victory
She became a spiritual leader of the French Resistance, demonstrating the right direction
And, when the war was over, her only regret was "not killing enough Nazis" sooner.

don david Calderon y. Aroesty
Undated, circa 2017

Why is Nancy Grace Augusta Wake Fiocca, Amazing Grace
In this book of Holocaust remembrances?
She is not Jewish, was not nominated to be a "righteous Gentile"
Did not focus her anti-Nazi efforts specifically on saving Jews
It is because the enemy of our enemies sometimes serves as our best friend
Moreover, her anti-Nazism was in part molded in Vienna
When she saw and was revolted by gangs of Nazis terrorizing Jews
In her final years in England, though she had other choices
She chose to live in a senior residence exclusively for war veterans
At all times, she had, she was, she epitomized amazing grace

Nightmares

The lawyer asked the Lady
Asked her what she wanted
I have a question, she said
A question about my Will

That's not my area, he said
Not really my area of expertise
But, go ahead, please ask me
I'll try my best to answer you

I have two children, two,
She told the lawyer, empathically
I was born in France, you know
Yes, the lawyer said, he knew

The Nazis took many of us early in the war
They stuffed us on a train in cattle cars
Took us to a place in southern Germany
It was ugly, cold and completely insufficient

Insufficient for human habitation,
They did not kill us, not then, not there, not right away
Apparently, the Nazis weren't ready, later they would be exporting us
Many miles east, it was the beginning, before they had their mechanisms

In the beginning, some of us escaped, not many, but a few who dared
Escaping, I found myself alone with a minor little group
A group of mostly German Jews, only one other Frenchman
He, his daughter and me were very much afraid, afraid of everyone, everything

The lawyer was interested, intrigued, but fidgety
The lady was a client's mother-in-law, he had to
Had to, treat her respectfully, what was she going to say
Wondering, he was, what could he possibly answer her

He steeled himself, acted patiently
She continued, "most of those in our little group
were adult men, all still dressed in their dirty train clothes,"
"It was before the striped uniforms; I was innocent, a virgin girl, 19"

"The Frenchman held his child, a tiny little girl,
A tiny little girl, maybe only six months old back then,
He clutched his baby girl, there was no wife in sight
'I'm running' he told me, we were each all running for our lives"

That's how I met my husband, my husband to be
We made it out of there, fortuitously, not directly
Eventually, we managed to get to neutral Switzerland
She is my daughter, that little one, she is mine

The lawyer gulped, the lady continued
"So, let me ask you, lawyer man
When it says here, in the Will, that
That I leave everything to my children"

"To my children, per stirpes, whatever does that mean"
"We waited to get married, until after the war was over
And he was absolutely sure and totally certain
That his first wife had not survived; we did not know until he knew"

We were married for forty-seven years, until he passed
There were many, many tears, some of them for joy
I feel lucky, we were very, very lucky to have escaped initially
Lucky to have her, our daughter, and then a boy, after the war

But continuing after the war, there were many nightmares
Nightmares, which happened, recurred repeatedly
In them, the authorities are coming after me, to punish me
To take back his daughter, my daughter, from me
And more recently, all my per stirpes grandchildren too

don david Calderon y. Aroesty
October 16, 2017

This specific story is partly allegorical; not really true
There is no doubt about the facts, however, the simple truths
The Nazis killed many, many entire Jewish families
They destroyed and disrupted many other Jewish families
Leaving young spouses prematurely as widows/widowers
Many children, as orphans or half orphans needing parents or foster parents
Survival was a struggle, and the struggles at times continued long after survival
They had to convince themselves they were entitled to life, liberty, happiness
In addition to millions of murders, the Holocaust blackened dreams of a generation
Requiring many souls to stretch for joys beyond the recurring nightmares

The Priest

It was June of 1942
The murder of the Jews in the Kraków ghetto was ongoing
Thousands were being deported to the Belzec death camp
Hundreds more were being murdered on the streets of the ghetto itself
Small children in the ghetto were especially vulnerable
They were dying of disease, starvation and selection for deportation

The family of Moses and Helen Hiller were trying to save their infant son
They exhausted every possible avenue of rescue for little Shachne
Failing all other alternatives, they begged Christian friends
Mr. and Mrs. Yachowitch, to please, take him in, hide him
It was an enormous favor which the Hillers were asking of them
Hiding Jews was a capital offense in Nazi occupied Poland
Anyone found hiding a Jew could be, would be, shot on sight

The Yachowitch family agreed to take the little boy, righteously
Their days and nights were full of risk and perils of being found out
To avoid suspicion, they moved to a different home in a different town
They feared that unfriendly suspicious neighbors might turn them in
Betray them to the Gestapo, hiding the little boy required great sacrifice
And came with enormous tension; nonetheless Mrs. Yachowitch grew to love the boy
and came to think of him almost as if he had been her birthed son

They had accepted responsibility for the two-year-old with a letter
Entrusting them and asking them to bring him up righteously
Righteously, as a Jew and to return him to his people, as a Jew
If when the madness ended, in the event the parents did not survive
Mr. and Mrs. Hiller did not survive, in March of 1943, the entire Kraków ghetto
and the adjacent work camp were liquidated; all were sent to Plaszow or Auschwitz

To properly hide the boy, Mrs. Yachowitch and he never missed a Sunday church service
To pretend to be Catholic, one has to participate in Catholic religious ceremonies
Shachne pretended well, he learned the hymns and as he grew, knew them all by heart
His big, bright eyes were alert, his mind inquiring, learning all that there was to know
After the war, with the world still simmering, conditions for Jews were surely unsure
Mrs. Yachowitch took him to the Priest, she was inclined to have him baptized
To make him into a real full-fledged Catholic, beyond question, beyond Nazi risks

Beyond neo-Nazi tricks and risks, to make him safe, she needed blessings from a Priest
She went to see the local Priest, a young, newly ordained parish Priest
She revealed to him the child's true identity and the circumstances of her custody of him
The young Priest refused to perform the baptism, explaining thoughtfully
To Mrs. Yachowitch, that it would be unfair and inappropriate under Catholic law
For him to assist her in violating the terms of the entrustment of the boy to them

It was, the Priest solemnly declared, the duty of the Yachowitches, to give the child back
If there was any hope at all, that Jewish relatives of the Hillers would take the child back
It was difficult to work out, but Mrs. Yachowitch did search and manage to succeed
To find and contact Canadian and American relatives, then return Shachne to them
The parting from the loving arms and hands of the Yachowitch family was painful
They had hid him thoughtfully, carefully, quietly, at risk of their own lives
Now, they were giving him away lovingly, but almost as if he had never been family

Little Shachne (Stanley) did not want to go, but when he went, he prospered
In his new environment, always without forgetting those who'd held him tightly
Close to themselves, when holding him tightly was the difference of life and death
He was educated in American universities, succeeded in the business world
And, also, became an observant Jew as his parents had prayed for him
But, the impenetrable bond he had with Mrs. Yachowitch never ceased to be

In October of 1978, something happened which caused these memories to be recalled
Mrs. Yachowitch, elderly by then, wrote Stanley a letter, a confession of sorts
In which she revealed to him, her long before prior inclination to baptize him as Catholic
And the good fortune she had when the young, and wise, Priest had told her not to do so
Insisting that the right and proper course for his and her personal righteousness
Was for the Yachowitch family to respect the boy's Judaism, return him to his people

The letter went on to say that
That priest had become Cardinal Karol Wojtyla of Kraków, Poland
Cardinal Karol Wojtyla of Kraków Poland was selected by the College of Cardinals
On October 16, 1978, he was selected to serve as Pope of all the Catholic people.[1]

don david Calderon y. Aroesty
April 1, 2019

Pope John Paul II was the first non-Italian Pope in several hundred years
He served the Church faithfully and well from 1978 to his sudden death in 2005
He traveled to the four corners of the Earth to expand his pilgrimage
He carried messages of faith and hope wherever he went, respectfully.
Few knew and understood that his messages of respectful faith and hope
Long predated his appointment as a Cardinal and his election to serve as Pope

---

[1] *Full credit to "The Merit of a Young Priest" in *Hasidic Tales of the Holocaust* by Yaffa Eliach (Oxford University Press, New York).

Voices and Echoes for the Unheralded

It was painful
It was painful to be Jewish in Poland, in 1939
It was painful to be Polish in Poland, in 1939
And, after 1939, it got worse, much worse, for both groups

From the inception of the Nazi occupation of western Poland
Jewish children were banned from attending school
Jews were barred from most employments
Jewish families were required by circumstances to be scavengers for food
There was a history of anti-Semitism in that part of the world

In the occupation, poor Polish farmers and others with only vegetable gardens
Found themselves competing with the starving Jews for survival rations
Even in the smallest Polish towns, those with a history of pogroms and those without
It was very hard for them to avoid confrontations; plus the Nazis had warned the Poles
Warned the Poles not to ever, never to, cooperate with the Jews, assist them in any way

They made it a crime, a criminal offense, punishable by punishments worse than death
To aid or assist any Jews, and they often carried out horrific punishments
The whole family of the offender being shot on the spot, in the street for all to see
There were more than 3.3 Million Jews in Poland when the war began
In 1942, the mass orders began directing all Jews, to report to railway stations
The Nazis were packaging them for transportation "elsewhere"

There were death camps in Poland even before Treblinka and Auschwitz were completed
To enforce the Nazi plan, the final solution, mass murder, absolute total annihilation
Physical elimination of all the Jews, eradicating thousands upon thousands,
Accumulating to millions; for most, there was no place to hide, desperate to survive

Hiding in plain sight was an impossibility for almost all of them
Jews stuck out, most, many, with their black hats, somber dress, and Yiddish language
They needed friends, friends willing to risk their lives, their everything
In Eastern Europe, many would not help, could not help, did not help,
Others, in addition, were plainly unsympathetic, bias is a contagious disease

105

So, it took a very exceptional gentile person, to stand out, outstandingly
With a willingness to do something, to lend a hand, to give directions, to provide
One potato or two, or a place to hide, shelter from the violence, one night or two
There were exceptions, bravely, those who risked their lives, everything, for strangers
The war continued, and when the Nazis won or lost battles, the Gestapo upped the ante
And, multiplied, magnified their efforts to capture and kill every Jew and Jew abettor

Fred K is a holocaust survivor, and like the others, he has a story to tell
He was born in Krakow, Poland, in April of 1940, the worst of times
The first and only child of loving parents, loving parents also trying to survive
They had been compelled to live in the Krakow ghetto until 1943
Towards the end of '43, they escaped, initially within Krakow, Poland

Fred K's father was a businessman and his mother a blonde, Polish in appearance
They passed, and they understood, that their lives depended on a further farther removal
They escaped again, this time, they paid mountaineers to take them, and five others
Over the mountains eastward to Slovakia, where they settled in a village
They made it on their own into Slovakia, but strangers on their own were unlikely
Unlikely to survive for any period, in Slovakia, or anywhere the Nazis roamed

They were then aided and assisted by an unlikely hero who appeared out of nowhere
He was a security guard and a state police officer, Josef Novovsky, and his wife, Mery
Knowingly looked the other way, befriending Fred K's family, protecting them
They made believe, pretended, looked the other way, went to church together
Novovsky helped them get along for as long as necessary, with the Nazis all around

Fred K has a child's memory of innocence about this man; Pepo his nickname,
He remembers him as hero and his wife, Mery, as heroine, throughout the war years
Inevitably, they were told, they likely knew, they were, had been, protecting Jews
Pepo proved to be a friend, a man of decency, honesty, compassion and respect
A man deserving for his personal courageous efforts for Fred K and his family

As the German Nazis began losing the war generally, they never retreated from their hate
Even while withdrawing from Poland, Slovakia and the eastern end of their occupations
They accelerated the Nazi efforts to murder Jews; they worked the ovens overtime
Pepo and Mery remained as protectors for Fred K's family; he remembers Mery specially
He remembers her holding his hand, while keeping him and his family safe throughout
the terrible trauma and turmoil; living through it, surviving was a difficult trick
Without Pepo and Mery it would have been impossible, simply undoable.

don david Calderon y. Aroesty
April 25, 2019

Many years later, Fred K, as an adult, wrote to Yad Vashem
Seeking to have Pepo and Mery recognized as righteous gentiles
Righteous persons who had risked their lives and their everything
to do the right thing; Fred's petition was declined because he had only been a child
So his father joined in the 2nd petition made, with no opposition
Again, declined because the evidence, they said, was insufficiently convincing
Also, Pepo was a police officer for a Fascist state, which made him more courageous
Not less, riskier for him and Mery to do what they did, for Fred K and family
Pepo and Mery passed away while the 3rd petition was pending, unresolved
The third rejection was because they were dead, unavailable to answer questions
There lies an important lesson in the rejections Fred K received; For every person
Recognized in Yad Vashem, there are likely many others whose heroic acts and heroism
did not meet the test in time; the unheralded also need voices and echoes.

Berga und Elster

US General Issue (GI) servicemen, GI Joes,
Draftees mostly, some volunteers, they knew they had to go
Their turn was coming anyway, good kids and nice young men
Joined in, this was a fight which had to be won, they came from ocean to ocean
From the cities and the prairies, they lined up with the regulars and the officers
They went to war with the most honorable of intentions, largely under prepared

Post Pearl Harbor, many joined immediately enthusiastically, to get back at the Japs
Who did the dirty deeds, and Hitler gave them no option, Germany declared war first
It was to be, there was no choice, a two front battle, in which we agreed to serve
Emotionally, they got ready to fight the fascistic enemies, according to the rules
In basic training, our men were taught something sounding like the Geneva rules
In case, in the event, they were ever taken prisoner, they had certain entitlements

Food and water, safe and clean housing, no abusive questioning
In retrospect, there was great naivete, blue skies and unreal expectations. though
The Germans tried, in many of the POW Camps, to treat the English and the Yanks
Respectfully, official military respecting official military on the other side
But Berga und Elster was a different kind of camp, it was a slave labor camp for POWs
Where a few hundred of the good kids and nice young men, were selected for Nazi treats

They were selected for special treatment by the Nazi bums and scum who ran the place
They were singled out for "looking like Jews," ""sounding like Jews"
Being trouble makers or simply "undesirables," they were met with Nazi indifference
"1st OK" in that place to beat and starve the inmates, to enforce hard labor rules
To emaciate them, those young American men, to the bone, to march them to death
Or right up to the point of death's door, before burying them in unmarked graves

Few in the American military knew; no one announced it during the war
That there were American servicemen, some of our own GI Joes, being treated
That way, the ones captured and imprisoned at *Berga und Elster*, within Germany
No, it wasn't the same as Auschwitz and Treblinka, no gas chambers or incinerators
No less a death camp, burials without tombstones, secret victims of the Holocaust
All of our GI Joes were heroic, those who were captured and held at *Berga und Elster*
Even more so, those who made it and those whose bodies were recovered from 7 mass graves,
US Servicemen; Good kids and nice young men, all of them, a small piece of
Just added evidence of the mass indecencies arising from official Nazi perversions

don david Calderon y. Aroesty
April 23, 2009

Berga an der Elster was a subdivision of the Buchenwald concentration camp
In violation of the provisions of the Geneva Convention, American prisoners were
Used as slave laborers, many died from malnutrition, pulmonary disease,
Mistreatment and beatings, including at least 73 American servicemen, plus
An additional 36 who fell during a forced march at the very end, April, 1945

OVER THE RAINBOW

Full Circle

The wheel of a bicycle is a full, entire circle
It doesn't really work, unless it is a full entire circle

Gino Bartali, an Italian, was a world class cyclist
Before the war, he won the Giro d'Italia long distance cyclist race twice
In 1936 and 1937, and he won the prestigious Tour de France, in 1938
After the war, he was champion in each of those events one more time

But, it was during the war that he did his most important and impressive pedaling
He performed spectacularly courageously and it wasn't a question of a competition
He, the iron man of Tuscany, used the pretense of many training runs inside of Italy
To help ferry documents and photographs, throughout Italy, to help out Italian Jews

Brother Italian Jews, not relatives of his, relatives of all Italians, needing to escape
He stuffed those documents and photographs inside the frame of his bicycle
Before he took it on those very long rides, waving gaily along the way
To the fascist, racist, Nazi soldiers there looking out for Jews and Jew abettors

Admiring his speedy cycling feats, those soldiers smiled, and waved back at him, even as
He carried the materials to an underground network of priests, nuns and other activists
All of them intending to help other Italians evade and escape the impact of the Holocaust
By creating false identifications and lying passports enabling those Jews to getaway

In 2-0-1-8, in honor of Gino Bartali, in a sense to pay him back, returning full circle
The first three days of the twenty-one day Giro d'Italia were held in Israel
It was the first time in the 101-year history of the Giro d'Italia, that the race did start
Outside of Italy, outside all of Europe, acknowledging a very righteous Italian humanist

Gino Bartali used his skills and risked his life to answer in his own rightful forceful way
Those who misconceived, and misunderstood, that minding one's own business
would, could, ever be sufficient when evil doers were infecting the entire hemisphere
Ferrying documents was not enough; Bartali also hid a Jewish family in his apartment.

don david Calderon y. Aroesty
May 5, 2018

It would be a large historical mistake to whitewash the Italian fascist anti-Semitism
Even before Italy entered the war on the side of Germany, its super-nationalistic
Haters were promulgating restrictive measures against their Jewish brethren
Thousands were displaced, chased away, and some later sent to the Polish camps

All of Italy has never come forward to account for those transgressions
That they happened to the extent that they happened makes the Gino Bartali
story even more important, more dramatic, an exclamation point in the center
Of the circle; Gino Bartali was a heroic figure in pre-WWII Italy
He had been interviewed by Mussolini, who saw him as a paragon of Fascist values,
He was an exhibit in Mussolini's proof that Italians were part of the "master race"

Bartali himself totally rejected Fascism and opposed anti-Semitism
He was far from alone in Italy; after the German occupation of Italy in 1943
Many Italians, including Roman Catholic priests, risked their lives to hide Jews
My Italian Secret: The Forgotten Heroes is a 2014 documentary film

The Forgotten Heroes is the story of the rescue of thousands of Italian Jews
Almost 90 percent of Italian Jews, including the family of Giorgio Goldenberg,
personally hidden by Gino Bartali, survived in Italy during WWII,
Thanks to the true Italian patriots and patriotism
They were believers in Italy, decency and ultimately democracy
It was because of them that Italy changed course in the middle of the war
Italy joined with the Allies and against the German Nazi axis.

Garden of Jars

We'll never fully know
How heroes come to be
An ordinary woman
A Polish social worker
A simply sincere smile
And, grandmotherly manner

Secretly, a mastermind
Saving children, the innocents
When few others dared to care
She took in many of them
From the Warsaw ghetto
While few others dared to care

She smuggled them out
Gave them a chance
Almost, a random chance
To survive, to live, to live a life
Minor miracles, many of them
Why they were the ones, we'll never know

Looking back, all we can picture is
Her simply sincere smile
A grandmotherly manner, masking
Her incomparable and courageous righteousness
The "right to life" to Irena Sendler
Was never merely a campaign slogan.

She saved the records
Of the children she saved
And placed in Christian homes
In jars she buried in the garden
So that she and others would never forget
That they were, would always be, Jewish

don david Calderon y. Aroesty
June 6, 2008

At risk to herself and all she knew
She, just by herself, individually
Decided that right was right
And the opposite of
Unchristian and ungodly wrongs
Irena Sendler died, honorably, on March 12, 2008.

GARDEN OF JARS

HEART OF GOLD

VOLUME 3

Adelaide the Saint

It was the Nazi period; perhaps the pinnacle of its ascendancy
The Germans had invaded France and conquered it easily
France surrendered, it really had no choice, it was surrender or death
The country was divided, Paris and the Atlantic region remained German-occupied
A Vichy government, Frenchmen compelled to collaborate with the Nazis,
was technically in charge in the south, adjacent to the Mediterranean

Dr. Adelaide Hautval, prior to '42, had no known political involvements
She was a medically trained physician, a psychiatrist
She lived in Vichy; Her mother had died in Paris, France
Under the rules, she required a pass, permission to travel from Vichy to France
There was, of course, no rational reason for her to be denied a pass

Bullshit, bureaucratic nonsense prevailed instead, the pass was denied
Dr. Hautval, being a proud French woman, elected to evade the rules
She had an obligation to her mother, to be present for her mother's funeral
They checked her out, stopped her, let her wait on the train platform, until
Another determination might be made, and in the interim she witnessed
German soldiers harassing a few Jews, a Jewish family waiting for a train

She spoke German perfectly, a byproduct of her medical education
She told the German soldiers calmly to leave the family alone
One of them replied "don't you see" don't you see "that they are only Jews"
She saw that they were Jewish people, then patiently, politely responded
They are people like the rest of us, she fervently added "Leave them all alone."
That answer landed her under arrest; locally, initially in the Bourges prison

A more senior German officer became involved and offered a compromise
Just "deny what you said about the Jews, and you will be released"
A simple proposition is all he asked, Dr. Hautval could say "boo hoo hoo"
"I made a verbal mistake" and that would be enough to satisfy the situation

The young soldiers had been trained in the Hitler years, 1933 et seq; they did not
see Jews as equals, as people entitled to human dignity, reasonable treatment
When Dr. Hautval failed and refused the compromise tendered, there was no leeway
That moment, she signed up inadvertently for transfer to Birkenau and other camps

She did not ask for that fate; She earned it by aligning herself with the Jews
As a friend of the Jews, willing to wear a piece of paper on her clothing saying so
Defending their human dignity was a capital offense in the negativity of the Nazi world
She was, in fact, a devout Protestant Christian, the daughter of a pastor
Christ was her teacher, the one and only son of God, crucified for His stubborn
Adherence to God's laws; and that also required her refusal to change her attitudes

In Birkenau, she was housed with 500 Jewish women prisoners
Using her medical knowledge and training, she treated many for typhus
By not reporting their illnesses alone, she saved them from death
The prisoners called her "the saint"; such acts of kindness were almost unknown
Unknown in and to the world of Nazi detention centers/death camps
In April of 1943, Adelaide was sent to Block 10 of Auschwitz

Block 10 of Auschwitz was where Dr. Mengele and others were experimenting
Using Jewish prisoners for often sadistic medical experiments
She refused to enter the operating room or assist in those experiments
Though sentenced to die, her execution was not carried out, instead
She was transferred back to Birkeneau, and more medical treatments
Of women prisoners with typhus, until Adelaide herself caught typhus too

There were other camps and medical assignments, Ravensbrück, Watenstett,
Ravensbrück again, until liberation in April, 1945 with the last persons out
She was awarded the **French Legion of Honor** in December of 1945
The **Righteous of the Nations at Yad Vashem** in 1965; and in the prior year
After Adelaide testified in a defamation suit about what went on in Block 10
The English judge declared **"Here is one of the most impressive, brave women
who has ever appeared before a court in this country, a woman of strong character and
extraordinary personality."** When the train of civilization goes off the tracks
It unquestionably requires people, many people, of strong character
To bring it back; To make clear that no compromise with evil is ever possible.

don david Calderon y. Aroesty
October 21, 2020

On an intersection in Vichy seeking a train to Paris in 1942
Dr. Hautval was unable to compromise with evil
Nazi assertions that Jews were less than human persons
It cost Adelaide three years in concentration camps and ultimately her life

---

In America, during the turbulent 1960s
And now, again, in Twenty-Twenty
Some Caucasian brothers and sisters
Have risen to the occasion, stood up for

For their Black brethren, African Americans
Emulating Saint Adelaide, motivated by decency
Black lives matter because all lives matter
Every single human being arrives naked and innocent
Endowed by our creator with certain inalienable rights
Equals, entitled to human dignity, reasonable treatment
Justice denied to anyone, by reason of the color of his or her skin
Race, religion, gender, gender orientation, or disability
Is justice denied to all of us, everyone, an unjust society
UNFORTUNATELY, NOT EVERYONE FEELS THAT WAY
SOMETIMES, CIVILIZATIONS RUN OFF THE TRACKS

Mythical Memories

My father had mythical memories
Of Monastir, Macedonia, the place
Where he had lived, before living in America
He didn't actually remember, he couldn't actually
Remember; he came here when he was seven years old

But, two older brothers came to America eight years later
And, in the absence of a better tutor, he became
Their first English teacher and New York directions monitor
In exchange for which, they reminded him, refreshed his
Recollections, of the old country, what it was like in Monastir

I know this only because I, his only son, no more than 9 myself, when I asked
What was it like in Monastir? Oh, he said, excitedly, some things were wonderful
Dinosaurs once lived there, he said; was that in jest, I still don't know
And, then, he added, that the moon sits on its mountain tops, you would
You could, he did, see it, when it happened, when the moon was full

Then, as I got older, there were more facts
Macedonia is a landlocked country surrounded by other nations
In history, they were jealous neighbors
Always seeking a piece or more of it; the wars were debilitating

Greece lies to the south of Macedonia
Salonika, once the Jerusalem of Europe
Lies close to Monastir, near the Macedonian border
Bulgaria is to the east, the Bulgarians are like
Complicated cousins, some of them were *Sephardic* too

Part of Serbia (now Kosovo) is directly due north
And Albania, to complete the picture
Is west, and then there is the Adriatic Sea
Which, separates the Balkans from Italy

Landlocked though it be, Macedonia
does not lack for topographical treats
it has a mountainous landscape
with many deep basins and valleys

It also offers two very large lakes, Lake Ohrid
Is one of the oldest, deepest and bluest
Lakes, in all of Europe, only a short same-day trip
From Monastir, now known as Bitola
Ohrid itself is a seductive little city

It's on the lake, emitting spirituality, it offers an old quarter
With cobblestone streets and magic geography
Built sideways on the site of a medieval castle, land of make-believe
Carved into the side of an ancient and very graceful sloping hill

My father remembered the Lake, Lake Ohrid
Because he was told it was so very blue and very deep
He remembered the nearby mountains too
They were cool and cold, windy, his family took the ice
From the mountains and carried it to Salonika

That was their business, family business,
That and carting fruits and vegetables too
Amidst the beautiful surroundings, the topography
Of Monastir, Macedonia, the place with the great lakes
Especially Lake Ohrid, with the Albanians on the other side of it

When, the Nazis came in force, in 1943, they wreaked horror on the *Sephardim*
The Yugoslavs, Tito & team, and the Macedonians specifically fought back
History shows that they explicitly invited the Jews to fight with them, as partisans
In the center of the City of Bitola, there is a statue of a girl, a Jew, who died fighting
She died fighting as a partisan, fighting for life, fighting for Macedonia

Maybe, I wonder, if it is me who has the mythical memories; no that can't be
Because my father and his *Sephardic* friends from Monastir, Macedonia
All followed a simple principle, it was absolutely necessary to befriend, befriend
Every good person one gets to know, and that is the essence of Macedonians.

don david Calderon y. Aroesty
2014, completed on April 25, 2017

It was in creative writing class
That someone first asked me
When I said that Macedonia was topographically beautiful,
What was most beautiful about it?
That is when I remembered, this then half completed poem
It was a question which tested my memory
As I had tested my father's memory
Macedonia is beautiful because, I said, because of
The lakes and the mountains, to be sure, and its wondrous ancestry

It is the people, mostly it's the people, who are the shining grace
Philip, Alexander, and other men and women, large, powerful, just and good
That to some, it sometimes seems that dinosaurs walked among the Macedonians
And imbued them with a special spirit, kindly, caring, generous and fair
Almost all the Jews of Macedonia were shipped to Treblinka on a single day
In March of 1943, a day of infamy.

Silent Screams

Marcel Mangel was born in Strasbourg
Alsace, France, the portion of France which was always in play
With many Germans living there, the territory claimed by Germany
And forcefully so, from the moment Hitler became the Chancellor

Marcel's household was multilingual
His father was a kosher butcher, Yiddish and French
His mother was a Werzberg, a native Alsatian, German-speaking
They lived peaceably with Alsatians of all denominations

Until, it was suddenly, the beginning of the Second World War and the end
France surrendered almost immediately, Marcel changed his name to Marcel Marceau
In order, one presumes, to camouflage his Jewishness
No one who really knew Marcel Marceau would have been fooled

He and his brother, Alain, were actively anti-Nazi
They served notably in the French underground
Among other things aiding French and Alsatian Jewish children seeking to escape
Marcel and Alain helped them safely, guided some of them, to neutral Switzerland

It was almost impossible to believe, impossible to imagine
One day playgrounds full with children of mixed ancestries and heritages
Running, laughing, playing games innocently with one another
And, then, on the next day, half of them, running, crying, badly needing to escape

It was a matter of life and death literally for 100s of French Jewish children,
Thanks to Marcel and others, some escaped and actually made it to neutral Switzerland
In the early years of the war, helping children to escape was his main cause and course
You'd never know, he used to say, which one would be or become an Einstein

He put his talents, as a mime, on display, only later, after the worst of the conflict
Starting with the liberation of Paris in 1944
He performed to celebrate the arrival of Charles de Gaulle joining with the allies
Marcel simultaneously working as an interpreter for the Free French forces

Marcel was a linguist, speaking nine languages, eloquently
Marcel was a mime, speaking no languages at all, equally transparently
He was expert at improvising human comedy, without a single word
His father had been shipped to Auschwitz, incinerated there

Marcel Marceau entertained in pantomime, celebrating the defeat of Nazism
The rout of the German troops forced out of France, the collapse of Vichy
Often, he appeared as a white-faced clown, who wore a silly sloppy top hat
He toured the world displaying his genius antics, making audiences relax and laugh again

While he himself was still silently screaming about the abusive disgusting Nazi tactics
The innumerable Jewish children massacred at Auschwitz and similar camps elsewhere
In his own mind; Marcel Marceau knew he had acted heroically to save the children;
His achievements were never enough, not for him, not for the many failed children

Behind his silenced voice, there was always the question in his arsenal of questions
How could it be, how did it happen, with so many responsible adults, many anti-Nazi
That we and they failed to stop it from happening, failed to prevent the limitless
Murders of innocent Jewish children, slaughtered in the slaughterhouses

Slaughterhouses mislabeled as detention centers or concentration camps
For Marcel. there had been nothing campy or amusing, about what went down there
After the war, Marcel often appeared as a white-faced clown, to hide his own frowns
Wordlessly, he helped. he tried to make the whole world recover and laugh again.

August 31, 2020

There is no answer, no easy answer
To the arsenal of questions the world still has, or should have
About innocent children suffocated and incinerated, turned into smoke and ashes
Made to disappear, swept away by history, almost as if they never existed,
Most left without leaving a single footprint or fingerprint, no one to remember them

Marcel Marceau offered the only answers possible for him
He provided boundless energy to get many across the border to safety
And then, he never forgot, always remembered, carried the memories
With him, as he performed as the world's best mime, silently screaming.

Anonymous

The Holocaust of the Jewish people in the period before and during WWII
A tragedy of unspeakable dimensions; and yet within that period, there were exceptions
It is critically important for us to realize, recognize and remember most of all
That the heroes and heroines who showed up were not all supermen and wonder women

Not at all, instead, the heroes and heroines who showed up, and did more than their share
Came in many different sizes, shapes, personalities and nationalities,
There was no cookie-cutter description, prescription for individuals with the bravery,
courage, valor, backbone, fortitude, spunk and selflessness to intervene

This one incident happened in 1943, in the area of Naples, Italy,
For seven decades since, Anthony D'Urso knew, he knew with a moral certainty
Knew that his own parents had been among those to answer a critical call for help
When such help was most urgently needed, they had responded, they had helped

Naples was being bombed daily nightly by the British and her Allies
Italy had not yet, but soon would, depart from its role with the Axis opposing the Allies
In the meanwhile, the German Nazis stationed in Italy were largely unrestrained
Their Gestapo were seeking, searching, frantically for Italian Jews, Jewish Italians

It was a rather remarkable situation and state of affairs which existed during those years
Mussolini had decided to be Hitler's friend and fascist partner in the Second World War
Together, they'd planned and plotted for a fascist German hegemony in Europe
Italian troops had been committed to the cause, and many had given their blood for it

At the same time, for the most part, despite the racial laws and prevailing bitterness
Some members of the Italian citizenry declined to be complicit in the war versus the Jews
Before the coming of the Germans to Italy, Italian Jews, Jewish Italians were safer there
Less perturbed, less disturbed, in Fascist Italy than most anywhere else on the continent

Young Anthony was only five or six years old when this was happening
The arrival, onslaught, of the Germans, with their bigotry and the Hitler hate agenda
Within the many provinces of Italy during 1943, the Nazis subjected the Italian Jews
To expropriation of their properties, plus extreme risks of capture, despair and death

Anthony's father, Giuseppe D'Urso. was a simple, straightforward man
He had no special education, no high degree of religious learning or philosophical bent
Giuseppe was a laborer and a caretaker for one Jewish property subject to expropriation
With its occupants subject to, subject to arrest and all the rest of the Holocaustic brew

Taking care, Giuseppe spirited that family, among other Napolitano Jews, Jewish Italians
To the mountains outside of Naples, to a secure place along a chain of alpine stables
Away from the Allied bombing attacks, and miles away from the German Nazi knives
Those self-sacrificing actions were taken despite the risks to their lives and limbs

When no one knew what the outcome of the war would be, they chose to act freely
A large number of unknown Italian heroes and heroines helped the Italian Jews
Many or most of those heroes and heroines acted anonymously, and quietly disappeared
They and their contributions to the causes of decency are unpublished, definitely ignored

Neglected and forgotten, almost as if those very brave acts had never happened at all.
Let this small note of praise for Giuseppe D'Urso and his family be like a testament
To the temerity of the extraordinary ordinary people who stood tall to the challenges.
To the anonymous heroes and heroines who stood up to the terrible tests of those times.

don david Calderon y. Aroesty
2019

The apple did not fall very far from the tree
Anthony D'Urso immigrated to America
With virtually no higher education
He attended night school to learn English
Then, went on for undergraduate and graduate degrees
He serves the community as a New York State Assemblyman
And, he is a volunteer builder of homes for charity
With Habitat for Humanity, he has served humanely
In Kenya, Haiti, and Nicaragua, he upholds the best
Of the best courageous values, in his family's tradition
His soft smile and gentle quiet manner makes him
Here and abroad, a goodwill Ambassador for America
When, whenever, there is a worldwide or local need
We all, we all, surely need more men and women of goodwill
To be heroes and heroines all over again, anonymously and otherwise

Hope Is the Last to Die

During the false peace
Between the Germans and the Russians
They pretended to cooperate when they co-occupied Poland
From September of 1939, when the Germans held the west of Poland
And the Russians held the east, and both sides likely realized it was temporary

The Germans were better prepared militarily and felt invincible
The German war against the Russians earnestly began in June of 1941
They planned for and expected to need a large forced labor camp for Russian POWs
They chose Lublin, a major Polish city, a metropolis, in eastern Poland.
As the place to build Majdanek, their intended forced labor camp

They broke ground for Majdanek in October or November of 1941
Majdanek's accessibility to Lublin permitted rapid construction
But, the facility was never completed as a forced labor camp; it wasn't necessary
Many Russian soldiers retreated to Russia, did not remain in Poland for the full fight
Of those remaining, history suggests that the Nazi's mostly didn't bother taking POWs

That's how Majdanek became, as it became, an early extermination camp
There were many, many, Polish Jews requiring final solution in Nazi terminology
Auschwitz and Treblinka were not yet completed with their gas chamber operations
Majdanek turned out to be the only Nazi extermination camp adjacent to a City
What went on in Majdanek was never a secret to the Lubliners nor to the Allies

Some people may say "they did not know" what was happening in the camps
Some people may say that they weren't personally involved with the camps
All of Lublin knew that the crematoriums at Majdanek were being used and
Being used to make the Jewish people caught in there to disappear
The failure of the world to blow the whistle at Majdanek was the beginning of the end

In November of 1943, Himmler was furious
Furious that there were still Jews alive in Poland
The Nazis brought an additional 18,400 Jews and other prisoners
To a central point in Majdanak, for their intended final solution

There were six crematoriums at Majdanak
They lined up many of the thousands of victims, in a series of long straight lines
Orderliness was very important to them, the Nazis

Orderliness is always important to men with small minds and evil intentions
Then they shot them all,. killed almost everyone in the lines, they fell like dominoes

During the shooting and the killing, the Nazi attendants played music, loudly
Marching music to cover the sounds of the screaming panicked dying humans
The victims fell atop one another, in a crisscross pattern, and then they put them
Put them in the crematoriums to burn the bodies to bone and ash for ready disposition

Halina (Helene) Birenbaum was in Majdanak, she was 10 years old when captured
13 years old when she was part of a group who had been brought there to die
Whatever happened happened, the technology malfunctioned and she did not succumb
In the Nazi era, who would live and who did die was often decided by the technology
Accidents and happenstance, who happened to be in the wrong place at the wrong time

On that day, when the technology malfunctioned, Halina Birenbaum was spared
She survived Himmler and Majdanak; she also survived Auschwitz
Very few survived Auschwitz, few survived Majdanak; fewer still survived both
After the war, she miraculously made it to Israel, and lived in the Jewish State
She became a wife, a mother and a vital symbol of our Jewish State, survival

Just living life normally was enough for most survivors of the Holocaust camps
It was not enough for Halina Birenbaum
She has distinguished herself as an Israeli writer and poet of great repute
Also as a translator and a citizen-activist in Israel
Her autobiographical *Hope Is the Last to Die* was published
In Hebrew, in English and in Polish, in Poland

don david Calderon y. Aroesty
Circa 2018

Hope is the Last to Die
Hope means you want "it"
It is the object or subject of the hope
The hoping party is uncertain of attaining it
In some contexts, it is a long shot
A parallel saying is "never give up."
It has religious significance
Some Christians say it is Christian in origin
Hope Dies Last, a Christian organization
Says that their name is based on a Russian proverb
As followers of Christ, they believe in the hereafter
Even when the human body fails, the soul retains
Hope of an encounter with Christ
Halina (Helene) Bierenbaum had her hopes for life tested
At Majdanek and Auschwitz and thereafter
A child, she was only a child, when she was subjected to

Nearly, practically, hopeless chances for survival
The crematoriums so close, they practically touched her skin
She summoned the courage to hope against hope
We too believe in God everlasting, and seek to be touched by him
These are not competitive belief systems; they are similar and adjoining
When the subject is one of life or death, Hope is a prayer for God's assistance

Hell

There is a Hell in the Hebrew Bible
Read Proverbs 9:18
"But little do they know that the dead are there
"Her guests are deep in the realm of the dead"
That's it, a place, Hades, deep below, that is the world of the dead
Occupied by all those whose souls have not risen to heaven

The Christian conception of Hell is much more vivid
Fire and brimstone, Hades is the deepest abyss
Where incarceration and eternal torment prevail
A place or state of everlasting punishment
Referencing a valley of Jerusalem, where in biblical times
Garbage was burned daily, fire and Hell were intertwined

The Nazis determined the Jews should go to the Hellfire
They merged their fatalistic fantasies of genocide
With a diabolical, mean-spirited, evil final solution
To liquidate all of the Jews in a lake of fire, burning them
As unrepentant incorrigible souls, reducing them to stubble and ashes
"All that do wickedly shall be stubble" waste remainder
"And the day that cometh shall burn them up"

Auschwitz and Treblinka and every other death camp
Were all man-made HELLs on earth, in every sense of the definition
Dragons and dysfunctional devils ruled in those HELLholes
The facilities were meager, insufficient for subsistence
Food was scarcely available, and if available, provided only as slop
There was hardly opportunity to breathe, none to breathe fresh air or experience life

For most all who entered those HELLs, their worldly existence would meet a sudden
Violent end, it was as if the sun, the moon and the stars simultaneously fell from the sky
The atmosphere inside of the shower room filled with stifling gaseous elements
Oxygen-deprived, brains ceased to function and their human flesh withered
The lambs of God were slaughtered by Nazi death's gruesome aides and accessories
Shoveled into open ovens where the flames and extreme heat decomposed their bodies

Hell, Hell, Hell, human sacrifice was practiced openly in those death camps
The murdered included men and women, adults and children, many children
Jews and gentiles, non-Nazis of other faiths and many others of different national origins
Slavs and Roma, among the many others too weak to fend for themselves, from them
The few heroic flesh and blood survivors cannot alone inherit the kingdom of God
It requires more; survival requires absolute faith we will all return to God before the end

The opponents of Nazism and those Hells on earth included many Christians
Ministers, pastors, priests and nuns among other faithful Christian believers
Some had read John's Catholic Book of Revelations
They were certainly familiar with the Four Horsemen of the Apocalypse
Prophesying a cataclysm destroying all the evil forces
They loved Christ passionately; ergo they hated Hitler, Nazis and Nazism

There were too few of them
They were not of any one sect or one nationality, some Catholic, some Protestant
Some opposed the Holocaust openly and nosily, others did so quietly, too quietly
Some cooperated with one another in any way possible to stop it, defeat it
Others acted in a lonely way, almost invisibly, without weapons greater than prayer
They were a strained and weak conglomerate against the armies of the Holocaust

Too feeble to win the day or get their way, they existed and exist
Some persisted throughout the war, throughout the Holocaust
Those disciples of Christ, when discovered and uncovered during the war,
were captured, imprisoned, punished, each as if a Jew, as Christ was too
They, those Christians, are among the people we are constrained to remember
The few miraculous survivors, and the exceptions who perished with us
We are required to remember them all and never to forget

don david Calderon y. Aroesty
November 21, 2017

During the era of the Holocaust, mostly Jews, but many others too, were
Dragged into the bowels of the Nazi death camps, few, against all odds, survived
Some survived with skepticism and some survived with their faith in God in tact
A keen sense of what to say to the Almighty if encountering the Almighty
They would, they could, they did, many did, later have such personal encounters

We, Jews and other faithful servants of the Almighty, are required
Not to be dispirited because those Hells existed, and other injustices persist
Resist, revive, energize, breathe the fresh air now and begin ourselves to chant
God is good, God is great, God knows us all together, as one human race
And, together we shall one day accomplish the goals of peace on Earth eternally

He Hid in the Woods

He hid in the woods
The child did
He hid in the woods, and he survived
The child did, amid very few of his kin and kindred family

The times were terrible, almost indescribable, even in the beginning of the war
It was winter in northeastern Poland, it was winter throughout all of the seasons
That winter was particularly harsh, cold, unforgiving, even your best
overcoat was insufficient, for the actual temperatures, rough winds and closed minds

The phony war had started on September 1, 1939
German planes had dropped a total of only two bombs
On his hometown, *Siemiatycze*, both missed their target marks
There were no visible signs of any Polish Army opposition, the fix was in

Of course, in the west, both England and France had promised war in retaliation if Germany
dared to strike; Germany struck and the English and French declared war
They were unprepared for it, it would prove to be a costly determination in lives and
otherwise, but in Poland, September, 1939, nothing, the German Army was unopposed

Twelve days later, per prearrangement, the Russians moved in, replacing the Germans
In eastern Poland, for the most part, comparatively, the Russians were mostly benevolent
They opened the schools, brought in teachers to teach the benefits of Communism
They did not bother building barracks for themselves; quartering themselves locally

The Russian infantrymen politely warned their new classmates and housemates
Warned them that whatever was happening in eastern Poland, under Russian control
was absolutely idyllic compared to the German activities in western Poland
Jews were being sequestered in ghetto areas, rounded up and worse
Feeble resistance efforts of the limited forces of Polish partisans were being squashed

It was June of 1941, early in the morning, when the German war in Poland really began
The German bombing of the east was voluminous and non-stopping, aimed at Russians
The German infantry was well-equipped and organized, they came driving in
Taking over, mobilizing everything, everywhere they could see, all to the last detail

The German Nazis were completely inhospitable to the Polish Jews, to say the very least
They also easily manipulated the political differences between their Polish victim groups
Making a mockery of the Jews, they told the Catholics; Jews had helped the Russians
They'd helped the Russian occupiers rape and pillage the local non-Jew Poles

The Germans intent was to prevent the Polish partisan groups from getting in the way
In the way of their intended ghettoizing and destruction of all the Jewish areas
Tough times are tougher still when one is all alone, without friends and allies to help out

From the summer of 1941 to the summer of 1942
For the Jews of northeastern Poland, in a staccato pattern, life became a wasteland
Bialystok was still the center, the main place for commerce and connections
Everywhere, the net was getting tighter, escape impossible, the end was near

With a mother who spoke German, Boris was hiding with a sister and a younger brother
They initially were safe, thanks to the help of a Russian man, who owned some buildings
Escape was difficult, survival after escape almost impossible, requiring great luck
And ingenuity, initiative, he scrounged for food, every day in every possible way

Initially, the cramped quarters in the abandoned old factory buildings, seemed luxurious
Compared to the alternatives: nothing, nowhere, there was no shelter from those ill winds
Eventually, they knew any place with a roof was destined to be examined, prove unsafe
They decided only mostly open air accommodations would facilitate survival maybe

Boris became the one in charge to find Polish farm families to let them live,
They sought respite in the recesses of the farmhouses, his sister and younger brother were
Not always strong enough to make it on their own, from farm to farm, each a hiding place
Together, they walked, hiding along the way, from the frightful fury surrounding them

In the fall of '42, the German occupation forces in Poland were ready for the next
Step, they created designated areas, ghettos, where the Jews were all forced to live
They constructed barbed wire fences, three meters high, to close them all in
The Jews caught in there, were like caged animals, awaiting their master's instructions

Their final instructions, liquidation was coming, no one announced it, all sensed it
In Warsaw, people later learned, the Jews in the ghetto revolted, put up a mighty fight
But organized resistance required organization and at least some weaponry
What was available in Warsaw was unavailable in most small towns, communities

On Sunday, November 2, 1942, in the middle of the night, the German
Sonder Commander, whose special expertise was liquidating Jews
Surrounded the ghetto in Boris's hometown, and began the process of liquidation
Shooting some on sight, burying those victims in large ditches, capturing the rest

The remaining Jews for the most part went compliantly, there was no reasonable Alternative, for
Them to see, that's how almost the entire population of entire towns
Ended up on the trains headed to promised concentration camps, certain death for most
Boris and his family successfully missed that fate, still hiding on farms during the days
And, mostly in the woods during the nights, Boris figured it out

Boris later found a farm to focus on, it was empty terrain adjacent to the woods
Mother did not have any money or gold to give to the farm family, but she offered
Something, a relative's old fine clothes, small payment indeed for the risks to be taken
The risks for hiding Jews were incalculable, betting everything for almost nothing
The tendering of the relative's old clothes made the farmer's grave gratuity not gratuitous

Technically true, but Boris did not take it that way, he would always be grateful to them
Survival thereafter required modern dancing skills, constant movement, fortitude
Amazing good luck, get up and go, the ability to foresee plateaus, to be wary and friendly
At the same time, to pass when passing was an option, to hide, no exposure otherwise
One needed to speak Polish and Russian, to understand German, and bury the Yiddish

Before it was over, near to the end, his kid brother was killed, shot and killed
By a German commander, an unarmed child, in the open road, he shot the boy in the back
A German commander, a weakling with a big gun, killed a boy without reason or civility
Boris learned of it, after the fact of it, while he was still hiding in the woods
And at the farmer's farm house hiding and surviving against all odds

Only 35 of the Jewish residents of Siemiatycze, 35 out of more than 6,000 at the start
Managed to survive all of the events, from the initial Russian occupation
To the, unbalanced, indecent German Nazi onslaught and murder of the Jews
Boris sadly said: "I cannot forgive what happened to my brother" and on reflection,
"I always think of him" mass murder makes murder banal until it is personal.

don david Calderon y. Aroesty
February 18, 2018, October 15, 2020

It is my pleasure and honor to have known Boris, personally, even if only lightly
Boris Kottler is a unique man, a true survivor of the Holocaust
He always smiles, never complains, wears natural body armor, sometimes
To protect him, it seems, against trivial things, life's miscellaneous grievances
Kotter, Boris, *My Amazing Life* Lifestyle Books, June, 2016
"Never forgive what happened to our brothers and sisters, always think of them"

To be touched by the soul and wisdom of those like Boris is inspirational
He had hid for his life in the woods of Poland and came out of that experience
With a zeal and optimism for life, almost beyond explanation, achieving
Many, many professional goals, including titles of great responsibility
and honor with US Automobile Dealers Associations

Learning of his personal experiences, his remembrances, were at the root
Of my reasons to assemble this small volume about other heroes
To remember them, all of them, as many examples as might be found
May we never forget them, and always recall Boris's brother shot in the back

The Nazi attacks upon us did not discriminate, between or among the Jews
Not between religious and nonobservant, not among members of varied sects
Not between rich and poor, not between the well-dressed or those in prison uniforms
There was never any entrance test for the concentration camps and no way out

Nor, did the Nazis favor those who lived in and fought for Germany in the first war
Nazis victimized German Jews, and those who'd never ever even been to Germany
All of them, all of us, became victims of the monster in the bottle, bottled, poisoned
Anti-Semitism; We are, we are, we will always be, brothers and sisters all.

MONSTER IN THE BOTTLE

Beneath a Scarlet Sky

In the beginning, Pino Lella wanted nothing to do with the war or warring
He was a normal Italian teenage boy mainly obsessed
With normal teenage boy inclinations, teenage girls, movies, and American music things

Italy was a fascist nation when WWII began, officially an ally of Germany
No one quite understood fully the whys and wherefores of it, though Italy surely
served as an ally, in Germany's quest and full intention to conquer the entire world

By 1943, the Brits were threatening to bomb northern Italy nightly when then
The Americans were on their ships offshore of Sicily, readying to come ashore
But, it was the Germans, their supposed friends, who invaded Italy first, armored tanks
Generals, thousands of strutting Nazi troops plus the SS Gestapo gang

In Milan, in May of 1943, WWII was raging, and the British had begun, had begun their
Relentless bombing campaign, so heartless it made a third of the residents homeless
And left every Milanese Italian shocked and scared, not knowing where to turn
That and other military snafus left the King, Victor Emanuel, shocked and scared as well

The King was not indecisive, in July he deposed Mussolini and had him arrested
By October, the King had broken Italy's pact with Germany and sided with the allies
Though the German Nazis had come to Milan assuming to protect the Italian Fascists
Once there, they were there, to do whatever they could do, to advance the Nazi cause
With little or no concern at all to the life and lives of ordinary Italians
Ordinary Italians, some starving, suffocating, many suffering from the ongoing conflict

Pino Lella and his younger brother Mimmo were sent away to school
To a Catholic boys school in the heart of the Alps
Casa Alpina, with its glorious views, just above Lake Como
Not too far from, within a healthy ski trip to, the nearby Swiss border

Pino knew nothing specific and definite about the Holocaust
Other than that the Nazis hated the Jews, until September of 1943
When those German Nazis rounded up 52 prominent Italian Jews in the town of Meina
Above Lake Maggiore, threw them in the Lake, and machine gunned them all

The Nazis left the floating, bloating bodies of the murdered Jews intentionally
In the Lake, for all the others in the town to see; After Meina and following the King
Many more Italians decided to become anti-fascist partisans against the German Nazis
Some also engaged in hiding and protecting their Italian Jewish brothers and friends

Pino was still seventeen and in the Alps to learn and to ski
Father Re at Casa Alpina had a secret mission for him to fulfill
He designed a program for Pino to train himself to be an Alpine guide
Intending Pino to guide many Jewish refugees across the Alps to safety in Switzerland

It was no easy task, Pino risked his life and injury to aid those strangers in need
Evading Nazi patrols looking out for them, surviving avalanches and icy conditions
Grenade attacks and hoodlums playacting the parts of anti-fascist partisans, while
Covering up their bungling ransoms. burglaries and tomfoolery

Pino skied through his vital role in the Casa Alpina underground route for the Jews
Pino did much more than merely lead his Jews, as if a shepherd and they his sheep
He often had to carry the weak and the elderly and to teach some children first to ski
Most of Pino's runs with the Jews took place in the cold harsh wartime winter of '43–'44
The Alps in the winter were never an easy pass; Pino passed with magnificence

Other people found out about this and other acts of bravery.
As a spy and otherwise, Pino never boasted of his undertakings
Made no claim of heroism; He said "he only did what he was told to do";
Of course, for sure, he only did what was asked of him by Father Re
As did many other, decent Italians of faith, good faith, and good conscience
Almost 90 percent of Italian Jews survived, survived the Holocaust and the war
It was safer for a Jew to have been Italian before the war began
Than to have been of almost any other European nationality

March 22, 2019

Based upon the book *Beneath a Scarlet Sky*
By Mark Sullivan who carefully explains in his novel of biographical fiction
That it closely hews to the facts which really happened as they happened
With Pino Lella, between June of 1943 and May of 1945
And it was much, much more than Alpine ski guidance for escaping Jews

He served the allies as a spy, while driving for a German General
He won and then lost during the fight, the lady he'd loved at first sight
That loss was a permanent stain and strain on him, his memories of the war

Though he himself did many good and gracious things, during the war years
He personally saw many bad and unforgivable acts, concluding
"We must have faith in God and in the Universe even if undeserved"
Pino Lella later lived a full and fashionable life, including as a Californian

Escape Route

One can never adequately fairly describe
The tension, the nervous anxiety, the silence and the screams
Chaotic confusion felt every day, every hour of every day
Brandished knives were as if hanging over their lives
There may not be a tomorrow, or any other morrow

It was in that chaos, that Aaron Abraham
Developed a route, an escape route
He prearranged it, just in case
Just in case the Germans came, when everyone knew
That they were already there and coming for the Jews

In the beginning, the English and the French together
Specifically defiantly told the Germans
Told them directly, never, not ever, to invade Poland
Demanding, they did, that the Germans respect Polish sovereignty
To do otherwise, they threatened, would mean certain war

Hitler laughed at the English and the French
Scoffing at their idle baseless ballyhoos of retribution
In 1939, Poland was not the German's true objective
It was only a stepping stone, along the way
Along the way to getting even with the English and the French

Aaron Abraham knew a route
He was a jeweler, a dealer in diamonds
A man of the world, he had contacts in the gentile world
From Moscow to Antwerp and places in between
Especially in Slovakia, he hastened to believe

The rabbi in Krakow, a gentle soul, compassionately
Asked Aaron Abraham to share his secret route
Aaron Abraham, in turn, respectfully declined
To share the secret would mean, it would not continue to be
A secret anymore, useless to him and all those planning to escape

The rabbi was displeased, to say the very least
His concern was not only for Aaron Abraham and family
It was for the entire congregation and community
Escape routes for everyone, all of his congregants, he wanted those
Each and all of everyone needed to know a route or two, some way out

Standing still was no one's intention
Yet, almost no one had the means to fight
Guns and other weapons had been anathema
In the Jewish community; to get along with the Poles
Nonviolent passivity had been a necessity to keep the peace
Aaron Abraham had had it with the status quo
The Germans were already there, everywhere in Poland
He was not waiting for detention, before acting on his own
When he felt the final solution on his neck, a minor step away
He, his wife and their baby boy, successfully escaped across the border

Before, before he left, Aaron Abraham had tried his best
Sincerely tried and failed to persuade his brother to come along
His brother, his brother's wife and their delightful children
He wanted them to come with him, to take the chance, as he'd described it
He remembers well, saying any chance was far better than sitting still,
With almost no chance at all; the time for passivity had passed

The brother and the brother's wife declined after thoughtful consideration
There was his mother and her mother, who would look after them?
Plus, they did not have the same means nor the same connections
There were so many Jews, the Germans couldn't kill them all, the brother postulated
The Germans would be too busy fighting with the Polish partisans to bother with Jews

Fully forty years after those events, Aaron Abraham was still carrying
In America, still carrying, in his wallet, a picture of a niece he lost
He had known a route, a secret route, for his and their escape
He could not share it with everyone, that was impossible
He had tried, tried his best, to save his brother and his brother's family

Many of the Jews who died in Poland in the 1940s died horribly
Many others who lived, survived, and escaped, died a thousand times
Unable always to fully understand, completely comprehend, they replayed the events
In their minds repeatedly, wondering whether, what, why, when
There was something they, each of them, might have done differently

For all of those others, captured in the vise of militant virulent Nazi theology
In the 1940s, the choices for the Jews of Europe were only to fight or to flee,
Fighting, for most, without weapons or organization, was fruitless and mindless
Escape by any means or methodology was entirely honorable, but for the escapees
There often was a terrible price to pay, never forgetting the terror, the pain, the tragedies

don david Calderon y. Aroesty, December 14, 2018

Name and some details changed to protect the innocent
No stranger to those events can fairly fully describe the survivors' scars
Post-trauma stress disorders are commonplace for wartime servicemen
Worse still for civilians dragged against their will to the edges of a burning fire
Then held there, or in hiding from, a force intending to exterminate them
Annihilate, blot out, demolish, and eradicate entirely those living human beings
Get rid of them as if they had never been, erasing them from the annals of life

The escaping civilians suffered stressful disorders of uncommon magnitude
Some made it through undisturbed, they were the exceptions,
More usually, the disturbing signs were always there, easily frightened and fearful
Plagued by anxiety and uncertainties which almost never disappeared

The devil's pictures, and insignia replayed and reappeared in days and nightmares
Aaron Abraham was a hero in real life; he overcame, escaped, got out of there
He and his entire immediate family survived and eventually arrived, in America
He overcame much, but not every memory; he kept his niece's picture in his wallet
Some losses did not go away, not ever, for the rest of their lives.

Fighting for Lost Causes

Fire, smoke and haze conglomerating
A constantly diminishing gloomy outlook
Dueling with only occasional rays of moderate sunshine
Hopelessness pervaded the atmosphere, losses prevailed

Noisy tanks trampled through the flower beds of Jewish life
In eastern Europe, machine gun bullets ceaselessly slicing humans
Other humans, perplexed, distressed, unable to move, unable
To cope, they considered surrender amid other suicidal submissions

While most of their fellow Jews were being murdered
Captured and killed or just killed instantaneously; giving up
Some Jews were searching for alternatives, including fighting back
Trying to do anything, anything at all to undermine the Nazis

They'd derail trains, burn bridges, sabotage communication lines
Destroy suspected collaborators, identifying and lynching them
"We couldn't really fight the whole German Army"
"We couldn't really, but we did our best to disrupt and interrupt"

There were not too many of them, clearly not enough, too few
To make a difference, even a dent in Nazi operations, but they did
What they did, the fighting they did, for the cause, for survival
For the idea and the ideals, for a Jewish nationhood, for tomorrow

The Warsaw ghetto uprising is the best-known example
Of Jews and Jewish fighting back, notwithstanding the lost causes
Or the impossibility of achievement, yet dreaming of it, risking all
A revolt by almost lifeless limited forces, ill-equipped to go to battle

Three quarters of a century later, the Warsaw ghetto fighters are still
Well-known and revered for the miracles they undertook and sought
Though virtually guaranteed to fail, the Warsaw ghetto uprising
Is a symbol of steadfastness, a stark refusal to submit or to surrender

don david Calderon y. Aroesty
April 12, 2018

Tanks may have trampled through our flower beds
They did not destroy the seeds, the seeds of freedom and urge for more, national identity
In Nineteen Hundred and Forty-Eight, after nearly two decades of Holocaust
Nearly Two Thousand years of on-again, off-again bigotry in lieu of brotherhood
Israel was born anew, Israel was born anew, a tarnished star rising up to shine
A child of ashes sprinkled with patient faith and a generation's resistance to obliteration,
Saved by fighters fighting lost causes during the Holocaust; they saved hope; each
And every battle fought inspired faith for the Jewish nation sought

Vladka's Students

Later, she would become best known for her students, who became her teachers, to tell the world
She was a living eyewitness to what had happened in Poland, in Warsaw, during the war
She published a best-selling book, in Yiddish, then in English, *On Both Sides of the Wall*
Undeniably a tell-all book, one of the first and best, most riveting accounts of the Warsaw uprising

She was born in Warsaw, raised in Warsaw, initially as a secular child, but she recognized
And realized her Judaism, as a teenager surrounded by the Warsaw Ghetto, she cut her eyeteeth
On the significance of her religious persona, and she was then the one to carry the dynamite
Which required boundless energy, raw courage and almost incredible *chutzpah*

She spoke Polish fluently, like a native, with carefully pronounced Polish slang uttered perfectly
Living on the Christian side, with a long-hanging mane of blond-red, blond hair, she could pass
Attractively, the Polish sentries gladly assumed her to be, then recognized her to be, one of them
They were sure, sure she was no Jew, a Catholic girl, entitled to passage to the Christian side

Her name at birth had been Feyge Pelte, she changed her name only when the difficulties began
She became Vladka, never to make believe, she would not deny her Jewish identity;
She was proud of it; she needed the alias to survive; she, we, all of the Jews in Poland, tried
Learned survival techniques; when she could pass; the name Vladka became her, stuck to her

Initially, she served only as a courier for the brothers and sisters stuck inside the Ghetto walls
She brought papers into them and could bring papers and other small items out, unsuspected
Reportedly, she was also at times involved in aiding some little children to escape; one time,
she carried out a map of Treblinka to agents for the western authorities, hoping it would help

The map, showing the instruments at Treblinka used for mass killings. did not earn intervention
The world still stood still, more needed to be done, that's the when and why of the Ghetto uprising
Only when there was no hope of help from anyone else, did they undertake all to live, to have
An opportunity to live a bountiful observant Jewish life, if possible

She married, during the war, to Benjamin Meed, another unapologetic resistant Polish Jew
After the war, they caught a Marine frigate to the United States and were enabled to resettle
They undertook the leadership of the Holocaust survivors' community in America
Vladka taught American public school teachers and Catholic parochial schoolteachers

She then took those teachers with her to Poland, and onto Israel
So that they could learn, and later teach to others, truths about the resistance and uprising
It is not true, never was true, that the Jews all simply merely obeyed and complied

As Vladka's teachers learned from direct eyewitnesses and participants,
They grew to understand the realities, the truths of the Holocaust
That's how Vladka's students became Vladka's teachers,
For what she did, before and during the Warsaw Ghetto uprising, and after the war
She is a living legend, a heroine in every sense of the word, bravery, courage and remembrance.

March 9, 2019

The Cap Arcona

Most every survivor, if asked
To thank God for his or her survival
Might well respond with a question
Directly addressed to the questioner
How can you believe in God?
If you really believe there is an Almighty
What Almighty God would have done this?
Would have permitted the Holocaust to happen?

Henry Bawnik was a survivor
A survivor many times over
As a child, he survived starvation in a Lodz ghetto
He survived imprisonment in Auschwitz
He survived transfer to other camps in Poland
Survived a ten day rail trip to Dora-Mittelbau
Which ended with the barely living souls
Dragging the corpses of others from the rail cars

And, in January of 1945, he survived The Cap Arcona
It was a Nazi trick in the Baltic Sea, just before surrender
They piled thousands of their prisoners onto the ship
The Cap Arcona, floating just feet from Germany
Flying flags with swastikas to attract the British bombers
It did attract the British bombers and their bombs
Crippling the vessel, sending it listing into the sea
Many thousands of innocents did drown, fewer survived

In 1949, Henry Bawnik, who miraculously made it through
Arrived in America, became an American
Lived a good life with a good wife for more than 60 years
They had three daughters, seven grandchildren and two more
Great grandchildren, survivors all of them
World War II pitted men defiling the injunctions of the Almighty
Fighting with others, observing the injunctions of the Almighty
How can one not believe there is an Almighty spirit, when
In the end, Henry Bawnik and his progeny miraculously made it through

don david Calderon y. Aroesty
October 12, 2018

Written for Henry's grandson, Jeremy Elias
Who took the time to do a private video of his grandfather
And wrote an article about the attack on The Cap Arcona
Which appeared in the Jerusalem Post cited
In Grandpa's obituary, *New York Times*, 9/12/2018

Why We Remember

It was January of 1945, the end was near
The Nazis decided to abandon Auschwitz
They needed to get out of there speedily before, before
The fast-approaching Soviet Army reached them
Found them with the living evidence of their crimes

The Nazis had choices with respect to the surviving prisoners
Regarding the disposition of the limited number of surviving prisoners
As hardened fascists, they could readily have shot and killed them all
But, that would have left bodies, additional evidence of their crimes
Obvious evidence of crimes to cover up the prior horrendous acts

They could also have left them there, all still alive, though barely still alive
But, that, too would have meant leaving witnesses, living eyes to the prior crimes
The Nazis had worked too long and too hard to keep their dirty deeds undiscovered
They had hidden their hideous acts from history; they simply could not leave witnesses,
Not dead, not alive, therefore, they decided, instead, ruthlessly, on a final death march

Death marches were nothing new for Nazis, they'd employed them previously
Hoping and expecting that each, and maybe all, of those barely surviving souls
Would pass, along the way, pass anonymously from unnatural natural causes
They expected them to pass, and not in one site, on the death march to Buchenwald
Those survivors were already starving, malnourished and ill-prepared
For a long journey in wretched winter weather, with barely any clothes

Most of them were already at death's door, before they took a single step
On the final march from Auschwitz, they were, in fact, intended to arrive nowhere
Virtually sure, almost certain, to succumb to exhaustion and other disabilities
Many of them, many of them in fact, did fail, drop and die along the way
No one bothered to bury them, the Nazis left the bodies as refuse to rot in the open air

There were some good and brave local Polish Christians who tried to aid the marchers
In one unlikely town, Ksiazenice, a Roman Catholic priest, Pawel Rys, a humanitarian
Saw to it that forty-five of the forced marchers who had been killed or died along the way
Were given a decent burial with a monument to mark their place
Given a decent burial with a monument to mark the place, and
Recording who it was that was buried there; Lacking names, the priest used

The numbers tattooed on their arms, the numbers tattooed enabled the authorities
To identify the dead and tell the story of the final march from Auschwitz to Buchenwald

The tattooed numbers were punctuation marks, evidence to tell about the hell
The monument Pawel built became the proof, exactly the opposite of Nazi intentions
Why we remember is a question for the ages; the need to remember is a clarion call Imprinted on our
DNA, we are who we are, we are all the progeny of the death marchers

don david Calderon y. Aroesty
February 18, 2018

Survivor from the Final March

I heard about him one day, unexpectedly, his daughter told me tearfully
Immediately, I went home and recorded the story I thought I heard;
It was important and relevant to this series of Remembrances I've written
I hoped I'd get it right, later she said to me, I got it right, the whole family agreed
As a young man, short and slight, no one would have expected
Predicted him to be the one, to have made it through, but he was one who had survived
Who survived the final march; there is something special about some people, very special

Joe was very special, everyone who knew him later on, would tell you so
After the march, he was repatriated and went back to his hometown in Eastern Europe
There, of course, was no one there, all the Jews were gone
His mother, his father, his sister and his brothers, all killed, dead and gone

They sent him on a Jewish orphans' trip to Scotland, for rehabilitation
Then to London, to learn a trade, the choices were very slim
Millinery, leather goods or jewelry, he picked jewelry, it interested him
Denied an education since before age 14, he decided to become a jeweler

He had distant relatives in America, he learned, thanks God
That earned him the right to immigrate to the land of opportunity, and so he did
When he arrived, not readily employable, the instant Yank instantly employed himself
He went into business as a self-employed jeweler and enjoyed a lifetime of success

His best success, he would tell you, was his beautiful wife and the beautiful life
They made together, for almost 64 years, until his recent departure, 73 years after
The final march out of Auschwitz, they have 3 children, 7 grandchildren and just
Then, starting out 3 great grandchildren, all of the progeny, implicitly, survivors too

Joe was almost always smiling, friendly, most interested most of all, in getting along
The children said, the doctors said, the grandchildren said, neighbors said
He was the delightful, light to their lives, a beam of sunshine every day in every way
Of course, he was, he says, as anyone would say, after surviving the final death march

The Nazis and Nazism selected every single Jew within their sphere for random death
Survival often was a matter of chance; surviving final death marches, determination
Some survivors, understandably, lived forever with fright and regret of the suffering
Others took the tack which appealed to Joe, constant celebration of life, love and joy
He lived to enjoy every precious moment and event; he was generous with his

Wisdom, spirit and material things; he and his brethren are the main reasons why we REMEMBER, never forget the sins and the horrors, always remember the positives POSITIVELY. **Joseph Moishe Zeller passed on March 3, 2018. His memory is a blessing, among our many reasons to remember, never to forget.**

April 2018

Behind Enemy Lines

She recently celebrated her birthday; 100 years young, in April, 20 2020
She has lived a full and intriguing life; her memory is as good as perfect eyesight
Marthe Cohn was a French Jewish ally of the Resistance during WWII
Near the very end of the conflict, she served in Germany, behind enemy lines

She had never told her story, not until the Shoah Project knocked on her door
But once they did, she did, she spoke up forcefully, rightfully, truthfully
She is short, diminutive, physically the antithesis of the image she projects, when
Talking about the events during the war, harrowing stories, her many narrow escapes

Beginning at the end, it was November of 1944, five months after D-Day
The Allied forces had advanced; Paris had been liberated
The German troops had retreated; they had not nearly surrendered
They were fighting back, fighting back feverishly, protecting their homeland

After liberation, the French Resistance regrouped, the French First Army was formed
The French First Army commenced an Intelligence Service; they needed spies
Eyes inside of Germany, to see what was going on, who could see what was going on
Where were the soft spots insufficiently protected, and places to avoid if they attacked

Marthe's maiden name was Hoffnung, it even sounded German, though she was French
She had been raised in Alsace-Lorraine; the border in Alsace-Lorraine was ever shifting
She herself had lived in the part which was German before, Germany remained
Right across from the changing border; She spoke German almost as well as her French

The Intelligence Service selected her, and managed to sneak her in via Switzerland
She posed as a nurse; nurses were in great demand, on both sides of the line
She was given papers and photographs of a captured German POW, enabling her
To claim she was looking for him, moving for the purpose of finding him, her fiancé

When she was asked to serve as a spy, she did not flinch, or need to think it over
She was willing to risk her life, to risk her life to help to end the war
To help to end the war which cost both communities in Alsace Lorraine so much
Her sister Suzanne had died in Auschwitz, as did Marthe's real-life fiancé as well

The Germans had erected a line as well, it was the Siegfried Line which no allied
Force was supposed to be able to cross; it represented Germany's impenetrability
Marthe was the one who reported back to the French First Army that the Siegfried Line

Had been abandoned, it no longer existed, was not an obstacle
German troops had been regrouped in the Black Forest

With that critical information, the French First Army successfully invaded Germany
She was hailed and applauded for her work; She received the *Croix de Guerre* in 1945
The *Médaille Militaire* in 1999; the French Legion of Honor in 2002, and you can't
Imagine this, she also received the *Order of Merit,* Germany's highest honor,
As word of her service spread in recent years; her German was as good as her French
She needed most of all, to end the war, which cost too much, too much in human lives.

don david Calderon y. Aroesty
December 27, 2019, May 11, 2020

The entire story of Marthe Hoffnung Cohn
Was celebrated by all for all she was able to do
Serving as a nurse on both sides of the line
Treating patients patiently, skillfully, hopefully
With a secret life, as a member of the French Resistance
Resisting Nazis, setting them back; and serving as a spy for the allies
Marthe married an American Jewish major, a doctor in the Army over there
He brought her back to California, where they shared beautiful lives together
Leaving her good deeds largely undiscovered for more than fifty full years

Uncommon Courage

There was a history of anti-Semitism in Greece as well
Some Greeks blamed the Jews because they had been brought to Greece by the Turks
From 1453, and the fall of Constantinople, since and now Istanbul
Until 1821, and the successful Greek revolution for independence
The Ottoman Turks controlled the entire Middle East, including Greece

Those were the same Ottoman Turks who sent ships to the shores of Spain
In 1492, to save the Jews, involuntarily departing Spain after the expulsion
Departing Spain to live and breathe and practice their religion elsewhere
The Ottomans placed the Sephardim in Greece, especially Thessaloniki
Salonika prospered and thrived for four hundred years, it was a new Jerusalem

The City burned in the great fire of 1917, and the relations between the Jews
Of Greece and the mainly Greek Orthodox Christian population
Was once again conflicted, constrained and difficult at times, and yet
The Jews of Greece were given full citizenship in 1920–1921, and when WWII
Reached Greece with an Italian invasion, Greek Jews disproportionately
Rushed to the fore, volunteered for Greece, militarily participated at home and abroad

Who is Zoe Dragoumis? And, how does she fit into this story?
Unless you're Greek, likely you have never heard her name
In Greece, Dragoumis is a famous family name
Ion Dragoumis was a heroic legendary revolutionary
Stefanos Dragoumis was a Greek prime minister in the early 20th Century
Zoe Dragoumis Palencia was one of Stefanos's four daughters

She was the only daughter who successfully avoided an arranged marriage
She was 31, late in life for marriage, in 1913, when she met Julio Palencia
He was a mild mannered, dashing, handsome, Spanish diplomat, a catch
He served the establishment in Spain, a man who played by the house rules
He was what she wanted, uncommonly for those times, a marriage for love
When they first married, he became Spain's Ambassador to Costa Rica

For thirty years, they lived a gilded life of power and prestige
Julio had many postings including in Shanghai, South Africa and Morocco
He and she were lacking nothing and yet missing something, they were childless
In 1936, Palencia was stationed in Istanbul, when the Spanish civil war was raging

The numerous Turkish Jews of Spanish ancestry, some with dual Spanish citizenship
Speaking Spanish, had an opinion about the war, and they were definitely anti-Franco

Julio Palencia had an opinion too, he had faithfully served the dictator of Spain
"Franco was always right" and the Sephardic Jews were confused and wrong
He did not say so diplomatically; he barked at them, with their "crooked eyes"
By 1943, the Jews in Europe could not concern themselves with bigoted words
Hitler and Germany were rampaging and in every nation, Jews were the prime target
A special target, intended to be taken, herded, concentrated in camps, and killed
The Sephardim had lived peaceably in the Balkans for more than 400 years
They could not, and did not, imagine mass annihilation ending their existence
They tried living with the threats, giving in, getting along, waiting for this to pass
In Macedonia, it did not look like it would pass, the Bulgarians were in charge
Allied with Germany from 1941, the Bulgarian civil authorities readied
themselves to send all the Bulgarian Jews and Macedonian Jews to the camps

After the Italian armies stalled, by 1943, the German Nazis had also conquered Greece
Zoe Dragoumis found out about it via news reports, and she cried
She cried and cried and wrote about the loss of a wondrous Greece, a place the world
would surely miss, and might never know again; She had room in her heart for the Jews
Julio was the Spanish Ambassador to Bulgaria, she saw the Jews in that region, suffering
She saw firsthand, in Bulgaria and in Macedonia, and she took it on herself to convince
Julio, the love of her life, to reverse field, get involved, to ask Franco to aid the Jews

Julio Palencia became a fervent advocate for the Sephardic Jews in the region
He wrote many letters and telegrams to the home office pleading for assistance
He wanted help for people who, though kicked out of Spain long, long ago
Had never ever abandoned the language, the culture, the music, art and romance
But neither Franco nor any of his many aides bothered to reply to Julio
On March 11, 1943, the Bulgarian soldiers in Macedonia acting for the Germans
Herded up 7,000 Macedonian Jews and stored them in a Tobacco warehouse

They were left there overnight, adjacent to the Skopje railway station
All of them protested, many cried, seeking freedom from their incarceration
Those who thought themselves entitled to protection as Spanish citizens, neutrals
Complained the loudest; but the Bulgarians rejected their claims
Spanish passports originated in Yugoslavia were worthless, they said, worthless
Julio Palencia wasted no time, he had the Spanish embassy in Bulgaria reprint
All of the passports they possibly could, 28 families, 150 persons were saved by Julio

In Bulgaria, the King intervened on behalf of all of the Bulgarian Jews
The King was too late, however, to save a well-known pair of Bulgarian brothers
Leon and Raphael Arie had been convicted of price gouging on soap and cosmetics
Accused, tried and convicted, publicly hanged in Sofia's town square within days
Bias has no time for witnesses or evidence, no tolerance for justice and decency

With uncommon courage, Zoe Dragoumis and Julio Valencia adopted the adult children
Of Leon Arie, and put those children on their Spanish passport for the rest of their lives.

don david Calderon y. Aroesty
April 29, 2020

There was more to the story than what was told, following the adoptions
The Bulgarians reacted forcefully to Dragoumis and Palencia
They declared them *persona non grata* expelling them from Bulgaria
The Spanish Government of Franco was also displeased
They demoted Julio and never again gave him an Ambassador's position

Or any discretion, in his positions with and for the Government of Spain
There is often a heavy price to pay for actions taken with uncommon courage
Julio Palencia, who had showed himself to be no idle friend of Jews generally
Understood that "herding Jews to the slaughterhouse" for no cause at all
Other than their being Jewish, violated the norms of civilization, civilized piety

Spanish civilization, he had reminded Franco's peons, though they wanted
No such reminder, Spain had been the home base and place of multiethnic greats
Giant minds and men, like Maimonides, Averroes and Ezra of Tudela
Julio executed his brave actions alone audaciously; Zoe provided the inspiration

When Julio Palencia died, Zoe Dragoumis, still angry with the Spanish slights
Had her husband buried outside of Spain, in the Dragoumis family plot in Athens
Where he still remains; Greece was the only European nation to vote against
the establishment of Israel as a Jewish State in 1948; Apparently, in Greece,
there was only one Zoe Dragoumis, She must be remembered as a special spirit

THE TRAIN STATION

After the Aftermath

After the war, Boris was still living. miraculously
Still living with the Polish farm family
The Polish farm family who helped to shield him
Let him hide on their property
Sleep in their farmhouse, some of the time

The dangers to the hidden were not over yet
Not entirely a thing of the past, in the aftermath
When peace was first declared and publicly pronounced
On Boris's farm, where he hid, two Russian soldiers, ordinary troops
Separated from their unit, making their way back home
Happened by the farm strictly by chance and requested
Peacefully, to be quartered there for only one night

The farmer and his wife graciously, rightfully
Invited them to stay and join the family for dinner
It was to be meat and potatoes, a celebration of sorts
They, the Russians, had defeated the Germans
Removed them from Poland, they had killed many Nazis,
Happily, at dinner, the soldiers recounted those events

Together, the group rejoiced that night, ate heartily
Drank vodka, sang Polish and Russian songs
The Russian soldiers stomped their boots
To the beat of the tunes, triumphantly, loudly
The alcohol having its intended effect, the soldiers
More than tipsy; there were broad smiles all around

Boris was there too, as a pretend family member
Boris heard the Russians say, significantly.
In one meaningful liquid toast, "Death to the Nazis"
"May they never come back" and that he understood
Then, there was a murmur, barely audible to him
Beneath the volume of the songs and boot stomping

Again, there were additional Russian words "Hitler"
Someone said "was terrible"; "Hitler was dead";
"The worst of the worst"; many innocents had died because

160

Because of him, in the battles at Stalingrad and otherwise
Then, the voice inflection changed again, as if it were a secret
When, one said: "Hitler had done us all one favor, though, one favor"

The Polish farmer nodded as if he agreed, gritting his teeth
Biding his time, not disagreeing or objecting verbally, vocally
To the sentiments expressed, leaving instead a small cloud in the conversation
A small cloud in the conversation, a pause, an invisible unanswered measure of doubt
Boris had heard enough, he heard what was said and he understood perfectly,
Silently he rose from the table, to clear the dishes and put them in the sink

In the kitchen, with time to think, Boris retrieved one of the Russian's rifles
He checked to make certain that it was loaded, it was surely loaded
Clicked the safety off, intentionally; he knew how to operate a rifle
He knew how to operate the Russian's rifle and definitely intended to do so
He intended to exact one small ounce of revenge for the "favor"
Hitler had done for them, and for the Russian's perception of it

The farmer's wife entered the kitchen too, cautiously determined
She approached Boris thoughtfully, kissed him gently on the forehead
And in one uninterrupted motion, removed the rifle from his clenched fist
"The Russians are our guests," she said
"The Russians are our guests tonight" she reminded him

Then, she added, "violence"; "violence even in a just revenge"
Would be unjustified, unfavorable, and contrary to our thinking
Contrary to the principles we share with you, adding "hateful words"
"Hateful words are only words"; "Nonviolence is required of our side"
"Except," she said, "to meet and defeat actual violence in progress"

The Polish farmer's wife was being very brave, though surely very scared
"I know I'm asking a lot of you; it is not my home that has been taken
Not my family that's been incinerated, not my life that's been turned into shambles
But no new order of merit will come from further disorder
Only decency, honesty and integrity will leave us, all of us, and you, all of you,
With an opportunity to prevail, we will prevail over time and with appropriate measures"

Many, many righteous men, responded properly to such pleas,
Even in the immediate aftermath of the most awful crimes history had ever recorded
Though revenge was merited and definitely rightfully due;
For the most part, Jews courageously abstained from random violence or vengeful acts

don david Calderon y. Aroesty
Circa 2013

Memories are complicated and sometimes conflicting
Before, there was no State of Israel; Now, the State of Israel exists
Those quick to criticize Israel for allegedly excessive zeal
Fail to understand or take into account, the extent to which almost all nations
All nations stood still, as if paralyzed, unable to help, during the Holocaust
Jews need to be their own protectors, Israel, the international guarantor,

Tolerance and Intolerance

This is a story about religious tolerance and intolerance
Both happen and sometimes they happen in the same place
Or with the same people, simultaneously or hundreds of years apart

Jews lived in numbers in Spain from the beginning
The beginning of the common era, when Spain was not yet Spain, a single entity
In the beginning, the Jews were farmers and fishermen
And, they were very happy to share in the common lot of their Iberian neighbors

The Spanish renaissance in Iberia proceeded well for several centuries
Until 711, when the Moors, Muslims from North Africa, invaded, initially
Conquering all of it, then stepping back and settling mainly in the province of Grenada
In the 10th, 11th and 12th centuries, more or less, mutual collaboration and coordination

It would be wrong to suggest any great democratic ideal was achieved
Nevertheless, the Catholics contributed their Latin knowledge, the Moors their Arabic,
And, the Jews threw in Hebrew, and suddenly surely Spain became the leading nation
The center of the Universe for advanced education, including sailing and shipbuilding

Wherever it was that the Spanish Catholics were governed by the Moors, they resented it
Commenced a war of *Reconquista*, intending to take back the whole of their land
The Spanish Jews with a history of dealings with both sides tried to be neutral in between
Neither foe nor friend, they became as if the volleyball in the middle,
perceived to be tactically, potentially, an enemy by both of them

In the midst of the *Reconquista,* some religious fanatics insisted on Jewish conversions
In 1395 and thereafter, conversions by mass attacks, assassinations, quarterings,
mean-spirited baptisms at knife point and required denunciations of Jews by former Jews
The intolerance continued in the 15th century with Torquemada's infamous Inquisition

By January 1, 1492, all of Spain was united and the armies of the Moors gave up and fled
King Ferdinand was the first King of the united Spain and Queen Isabella was his wife
They had important things to do, great opportunities for them and the unified Spain to do
They could not let the religious fanatics and their violent inquisitions be the all of it

One of the first acts of the new King was to, as he saw it, invite some Jews to stay
The edict of expulsion required all the Jews of Spain to convert voluntarily or leave,
It was hardly moderation or toleration, even though about half remained, as *conversos*
The other half departed, a large fraction saved by the Ottomans, in Turkish places

The Jews had been expelled, thrown out of Spain on only three months' notice
The expulsion was indecent, intolerant and inflexible, and condemned by the Rabbis
Who placed a hex on Spain, hoping and expecting Jews to stay away from Spain forever
From this once promised and promising homeland, which abruptly divorced them
Divorced them from their Jewish brothers, and from their once implicit Spanish brothers

****

Four Hundred and Fifty years later, between 1940 and 1944, in Paris, France
Four Spanish priests put their lives at risk for their once upon a time Jewish brothers
Seeking to save especially Jews of Spanish ancestry from Nazi persecution
During that four-year period, they forged fake baptismal certificates for many of them

The certificates were intended to let those people go, to pass, as make-believe Christians
As part of a plan and plot for them to flee France to go to Spain, then a neutral country
Thousands of Jews were caught in occupied France and Vichy; they sought to get away
The pressure to escape was magnified when Vichy commenced a Jew census (10/30/40)

The Spanish priests efforts and these events were unknown and undiscovered until 2018
When a 26-year-old Spanish doctoral student happened upon a 70-year-old secret
He was researching the subject of Spanish diplomacy during the Holocaust period
A history professor, it was to be his thesis at the University of Extremadura

In central Spain, Toledo is a pretty city with colorfully paved streets and thoroughfares
In the 15th Century and earlier, Toledo had a vital and resourceful Jewish group
And, back then, Toledo was a popular surname for Spanish Jews from all over Spain
Recently, the researcher, new to his project, happened to be meeting with Alain Toledo

Alain merely mentioned that his parents had reached Spain with forged baptismal papers
He said it matter-of-factly, as if it was of no great consequence or significance
The researcher, Santiago Lopez Rodriguez, was astounded and curious to learn more
Upon inquiry, facts were added, it was in a Spanish church, in Paris, the Claretian order

That's where the forged baptismal papers for the Toledo family were reportedly made
Lopez let no grass grow under his feet; he promptly took the time to visit Paris
He knocked at the door of the Claretian mission, and told his hosts why he was there
They were immediately forthright, "we have all the records" they assured him

And led him through a winding narrow passageway to a small closet housing the records
There, Lopez first relearned some lessons many history books had generally omitted

A strange thing happened to the Spanish Jews in exile after 1492; they became almost
As if *Espanoles sin patria*, Spaniards without a country, craving a Spanish connection

They continued their use of Spanish language, 15th century Castilian modified by idioms,
Ladino, ancestral Spanish, as Spanish as could be, saved by the *Sephardim*
Even generations after the expulsion, they retained fanciful memories of the motherland
A respect for its culture, its foods, its arts, its music, and its folk tales told anew

As the priests led Lopez through the long winding narrow passageway, and he came upon the
Closet, he saw it was filled with cases of copies of the certificates from the '40s
It was first hand evidence of dozens of forged false baptismal entrees in the 1940s
Written in blue ink and black ink, written by brave men facing great risk, fears and tears

All of the subjects had *Sephardic* Jewish surnames before being baptized
None of them were French; almost all were from faraway, the Ottomans
Thessaloniki, Greece and some formerly from Istanbul in Turkey, predominately
Descendants of families who'd lived in Spain long, long ago, *antes* 1492

1492/1942, the same digits simply rearranged in order
The same problems, threats, expulsion, nowhere to go
Excepting that the risks in 1942 were even many times greater and more scary
Only gruesome deaths awaited those who could not escape the Nazis in 1942

It took enormous courage, almost unimaginable creativity, for the Priests
For the Spanish Priests of the Claretian mission to overcome French church intolerance
and Spanish institutional indifference, to issue 155 forged baptismal certificates
Plus 22 forged marriages, circumventing the Nazi forces and their Vichy puppets

About one half of the beneficiaries of those forged papers made it back home
To be in their ancestral home, Spain, again, during the war and for years thereafter
On March 31, 1992, King Juan Carlos appeared in the synagogue in Madrid
And, there, he proudly revoked the Edict of Expulsion once and forever
But it was the four Claretian Priests, spiting in the face of the Nazi Holocaust
Who had opened the doors to tolerance, opened the doors to Spain in the 20th Century

don david Calderon y. Aroesty
October 29, 2020

Father Joaquin Aller
Father Gilberto Valtierra
Father Emilio Martin
Father Ignacio Turrillas, and

(Lopez noticed that the four priests each took turns forging the certificates.)

The Spanish Counsel General in Paris, in 1940–1944, Bernardo Rolland Joined in their heroic acts
In 1992 by King Juan Carlos and Queen Sophia, and Haham Rabbi Solomon Gaon, Yeshiva University,
    the Prince of Asturias Prize.

The record of the Fascist Franco Government
During the World War II years of the Holocaust
Was mixed, they stayed neutral, refused to ally with Hitler
But, never tried to save the Jews, *Sephardim* or others
While Spain allowed it's land to serve as a portal, point of departure
For thousands of others escaping Nazi terrors in Europe at that time.

Sr. Lopez has completed and published his thesis on Spanish diplomacy during
The Holocaust, which contains the amazing details about the Claretian priests.
Like their founder, Saint Anthony Mary Claret, they believe, in God's reign
Of life, love, justice and peace; We believe, we believe in God's reign too
He who opens the doors to tolerance, opens the doors to justice and peace
Universally, may it spread from Spain to God's reign anywhere and everywhere

ANNE FRANK'S CHESTNUT TREE

Pink Graffiti

In 2018, the fluorescent pink graffiti
Was boldly baldly painted on a house
Calling the house "a public toilet"
And identifying its former occupant
To have been an alleged "Nazi Jew"
"Living in Hell with Hitler"

The former occupant had been Elie Weisel
A Nobel prize laureate recipient for literature
Generally conceded to be a good and wise man, a symbol of the suffering
And, of the magnificence of his tolerance after survival from hate's explosion

It was his house, in eastern Romania
Where he had lived before the war
Before he and his family had been taken away
Taken to the train station, en route to Auschwitz, in 1944

Fluorescent pink graffiti emblazoned on the house
Calling it a public toilet, intentionally
For the writer had surely, certainly, defiled it
And, with his own instrument, treated it as a urinal

It is almost unimaginable that more than seventy years after the Holocaust
After the Holocaust had been identified as The Holocaust in which many millions died
Totally needlessly, there are still some people, of every nationality, many of them,
Not just a few, a significant group, who still indulge in fantasies of a world without Jews

They, who have not had enough of their addiction and infliction of painful intolerance
"Blame it on the Jews," they screech, the Jews were the ones responsible for the Nazis
Forgetting, of course, that we had formerly lived as peaceful neighbors side by side

The Pink graffiti artists should remind us over and over again of the incredible courage
Of Elie Weisel and his coreligionist brothers and sisters who came back from the hells
Then, summoned the strength, to answer back, to expose the perversity for what it was
What it is, what it will always be, the stuff found in toilets internationally

don david Calderon y. Aroesty
August 8, 2018

168

From time immemorial, as far back as history can recollect
Our left arms have been carrying our religion, religious beliefs, while
Our right arms are pledged to support our respective nationalities loyally
Dual loyalty has been misconstrued, misinterpreted purposely, to charge disloyalty

Charges written often in vile words, pink graffiti, espoused by pink graffiti artists
Our adversaries have the noisiest voices when preaching to the angriest crowds
Even today, they are spanning, spamming, spinning out of control, with hate
Challenging our right and entitlement to be here, there or in any nation or place

Spitting on us, because we dare adhere to believe in a single God, *Adonai*
We've been subjected to expulsion, exclusion, threatened with extinction, and
Against those threats, and worse acts, Jews and Judaism have persisted,
Resisted, revived, survived and thrives anew, emerging with our faith in tact

That is one of the most important lessons intended by these Remembrances
Always, be true to yourself and to others, fair and kind, and tolerant of innocents
Remembering the few who fought with the many to stand up for the Jew
Taking risks against all odds and in many cases at great cost, even loss of their lives
To distinguish right from wrong, to be strong and firm in every just view.

We're All Jews Here

"We're all Jews here"
Said Master Sergeant Roddie Edmonds
A good and decent Christian American
The highest ranking noncommissioned officer
Stuck, captured in the bowels of *Stalag* 9A
A Nazi prisoner-of-war camp in Germany

It was January of 1945, the war was almost over
The Germans were losing, it was obvious to see
In Berlin, the bigwigs were planning their escape
Those who could, would go to South America
Others would plot deniability, hiding or suicide
But not too late to send the troops on one last ditch effort

Madness, of course, so crazy that it worked for a while
The Battle of the Bulge was the Germans frantic defense
On their western borders; while the Russians were coming
Coming from the east; On the western front, in the
Battle of the Bulge, the German troops held their own
Successfully surprised and captured thousands of American GIs

The camp commander at *Stalag* 9A had an idea
He called for and demanded that the Jewish American GIs
Report to, and line up on, the parade grounds opposite the barracks
Master Sergeant Roddie Edmonds heard about that, and decided
He had a different idea, all the troops, every American
Would report to, and line up, on the grounds opposite the barracks

The camp commander thought it to be not a good joke
He whipped out his *luger* and put it to Roddie's head
Threatening to pull the trigger, and kill him surely dead
Demanding now an explanation, what is the meaning of this?
He wanted to know; the Master Sergeant did not hesitate
Simple, he said, here, in this place, "we are all Jews."

December 9, 2016

This is the true story of a valiant heroic ordinary American serviceman
His story is remembered in *Yad Vashem* in Israel in its hall of heroes
For he quite likely saved 200 Jewish American GIs
By his bravery and gallantry at Stalag 9A, with a German pistol aimed at his head
He understood the meaning of standing side by side.
I wonder myself when at the American colleges in 2016, the Beating, Dragging
Suffocation forces are belittling and berating Jewish American students,
Their classmates, where are the Roddie Edmonds people of this generation,
To demonstrate they understand the meaning of standing side by side.

BENEATH A SCARLET SKY

Overcoming

He had survived the Holocaust, he had
It was a miracle, of sorts, a story which made the news again in 2020
Though it had happened in 1943, April 19, 1943, to Simon Gronowski, a Belgian Jew
11 years old at the time, he was caught in a roundup of Belgian Jews in Melchelen
He and his mother were packed into a cattle car headed towards Auschwitz
Along with dozens of others, all of them headed toward Auschwitz and certain death

April of 1943, the shine was beginning to dull on the Nazi myth of their invincibility
In every captured country, partisans had formed into units fighting back
The train Simon and his mother were captured on, now known as Convoy 20,
Was attacked by three resistance fighters shortly after its departure
In the commotion which followed, many Jews escaped from the cattle cars
They made it out to the fields of Flanders, hidden by the height of the wheat

Soon after the disruption ended, the train started accelerating again
Those operating it wanted out of there, away from any resistance fighters remaining
The train was on the way again, taking another group of Jews on a journey to nowhere
Mrs. Gronowski, Simon's mother, urged her son to take a leap
"Get out of here" she said to him, urgently and persistently
"Jump off the moving train and getaway," she begged of him to do

He hesitated, wanted his mother to go first, not for him to leave her alone
"Show me the way" he asked of her, so to speak, but she was quite reluctant
Simon jumped only because he was a good obedient young son, listening to mother
He left his mother, because he loved his mother so he listened to his mother
He did what she asked of him, and he landed on his feet in the middle of Flanders

For many long months, he was hidden by anonymous Catholic Belgian farm families
Who hid him in their attics and cellars, farmhouses and other darkened sites and places
Their objective and intention was not to entertain him, but to keep him hidden
Out of sight, out of the way, beyond the scope and radar screen of the Nazi machine

Now it is 2020, and the enemy is of a completely different composition
It was the height of the first wave of the coronavirus pandemic
And, Brussels, Belgium was hit as hard as anyplace else on Earth
Many infected persons, many hospitalizations and many deaths

The worst of it for the fortunate families escaping infection, disease and death
was the loneliness, the absence of socialization, ordinary human to human connections
In that one way, it was symptomatic of the Holocaust to him, dark, cold and lonely
Afraid, in his apartment, he moved his electric piano to beneath his windowsill

He flung open the window, letting in the spring sunshine, and fresh air
And, then, he began to play, filling the empty streets with reverberating sounds
Jazz music replaced the somber silence for his besieged neighbors to hear from him
They heard his music; they knew it was something special, it reinvigorated them

Simon Gronowski had most certainly intended for his impromptu piano concerts
To make his neighbors happy, or at the very least, less lonely, less frightened, happier,
Music is a means of communication and connection, he'd known that all his life
His older sister, Ita, 19, who perished in Auschwitz, was a classical pianist

Playing the piano publicly in the earliest days of the pandemic required
Bravery, courage and personal spirit to overcome the ennui impacting all of them
Mr. Gronowski had previously proven he had the stuff to act for himself and do it well
As when he jumped off the train in Convoy 20, sustained himself for 17 months in hiding

When he returned to his empty family home in Belgium to begin life anew
When he graduated at age 23, with a PhD in law, met and married Marie Claire
They had two daughters and six decades mainly of silent tribute to his parents and
To his beloved sister, before he wrote his first book, *The Child of the 20th Convoy*

Simon Gronowski did not, does not waste his time in self-pity—he does the opposite
He overcomes what was done by "bringing something positive to young people"
While "it was painful to stir it all up again" "it makes him happy, liberated"
To have become widely known in Belgium, giving lectures, especially at schools

As a consequence of one lecture, he met another man of similar age, near 90 now
A Belgian artist, Koenraad, who had also written a book about the Holocaust
From a different perspective entirely: he wrote about the guilt of being in a Nazi family
His elder brother was a guard at the same Mechelen camp as Gronowski had been held

The two men formed a friendship, more than a friendship, a bond of brotherhood
The two wrote a book together "Finally, Liberated" and gave lectures together
And when Koenraad's elder brother, the camp guard, was dying, Simon met with him
The brother plead for forgiveness, and Simon forgave him, saying,
"This forgiveness was a relief for him, but it was an even bigger relief for me."

don david Calderon y. Aroesty
November 22, 2020

This entire story, almost every word of it, was in yesterday's *New York Times*
It was sent to me by a lady I met at Temple Sinai, in Roslyn, NY, a teacher, tutor
She teaches children every year about the Holocaust, lessons from the history
This story happened to reach me as I was finalizing the series of Remembrances
I had collected and written over the years, and I thought it to be an *afitar*
Afitar in Ladino (Jewish Spanish based on 15th-Century Castilian)
Means a coincidence which is more than a coincidence, so two final points emerge
Thank you, to all the volunteers who teach and tell the stories of the Holocaust
Thank you, greatly, Mr. Gronowski for your piano skills and for overcoming

Remembrances
First Appendix

In the inception of this book, before the presentation of the short stories relating to certain heroes and heroines who did appear during the period of the Holocaust. The author introduced himself and sought to explain the circumstances relating to his personal motivation for assembling this material. The first five attachments in this first appendix are embellishments on that explanation referenced in the second, third, and fourth paragraphs on page 4 supra.

Cardiac Arrest

- Second Chance
- Fortuitous Circumstances

Sephardic History

- The List
- March of 1943

Reunion with Spain

- A Brush with History

To those pieces, the author also attaches a small sample of "other observations" which relate to, at least, what he sees it to both the anti-Semitism and Anti-Israel bigotry that sadly still exists and also to efforts made to overcome. These other observations are lenses to help understand the author's outlook. Are we truly beyond the Holocaust, or is the world just taking a break?

- Cemetery Stones
- God Is Interdenominational
- A Would-Be Suicide Bomber
- On Charlottesville

Yes, we know prescient words might well have been added relating to January 6, 2021. Maybe, you will add them.

Second Chance

What does it mean?
What does it mean to have a second chance
A second chance at life itself
A God-given mulligan for humans
An awe inspiring, unbelievable, unexpected
Unearned, extra opportunity to do good, do well.

What does it mean?
A second chance means everything
You can hug your loved ones tighter
Bring them closer, and closer together
Even more than they were before
And, especially, to fix the fixable.

What does it mean?
You can, with a free conscience
Call balls and strikes, foul or fair
All, as you see them, unafraid, independently
Without undue influence, or petty bias and partiality
Nor, submission to overwhelming majority whim.

What does it mean?
With the same eyes, you will see differently
3D clarity, amplified and reinforced
You're reconnected to your past
And, newly connected to the future
Special impressions, wondrous expressions.

Properly guided, you may turn out to be
Wise beyond your numbered years
A second chance is a second chance
To learn, to know, appreciate, say thank you
Look intently to the sky, and really see the stars
If they twinkle, perhaps, they're winking at you.

The second chance is not debt free
You have another obligation to yourself
Your family and friends, and also to your saviors

An obligation to pay it forward
To do for unnamed others, unexpectedly.
Voluntary, kind, perhaps even awe-inspiring things
Announcing, pronouncing, it was no mistake
Your second chance was a fortuitous choice.

don david Calderon y. Aroesty
May 22, 2013

Fortuitous Circumstances

I am a very lucky man. Before 2012, I already had a very lucky life. I am born in the USA in 1940, the beginning of the American era. With the allied victory in WWII, there was the elevation of our national star among the constellation of nations; it was lucky for all of us to be Americans. In addition, I had good, loving, caring parents in a good, safe, ordinary, blue-collar household in Brooklyn, New York, a great affordable higher education at Brooklyn College and Duke University law school and then, additionally, Columbia University. A beautiful, loyal, and supportive wife, two sweet-loving daughters, one great son-in-law, and three amazing granddaughters. I also had experienced good to very good professional employments and engagements as a businessman and a corporate and securities attorney. Then, I hit the jackpot. When almost certain sudden death threatened, I managed to avoid an adverse outcome. My survival was due to truly fortuitous circumstances.

It happened on September 21, 2012. I was at the United Nations. I had been to the building maybe twice before in my lifetime. That morning, together with a business associate Mr. Stewart Cahn, I attended a presentation concerning the fate of Jewish citizens of the Arab nations following the creation of the State of Israel in 1948. While the displacement of Palestinians by reason of the disruptions in 1948 has long been, and continues to be, a topic of urgent interest at the UN, the displacement of the Jews from the Arab lands is a long-forgotten issue largely because Israel took them in, made them full citizens, and in the years since, has done pretty well, integrating them into a well-functioning and improving Israeli society. The topic, though highly interesting, was not what made the day memorable. Indeed, I barely remembered what the lecturer said.

Upon completion of the presentation, I, together with the rest of the audience, rose from my seat and proceeded to leave the building. I safely crossed 1st Avenue and turned right on 44th Street. We were headed toward a very nice restaurant. Likely, I was only steps from it and perhaps two steps behind Stewart when he heard the thud of me falling backward. I was down and out, Stewart rushed over to me and quickly determined that I had no heartbeat and no pulse. I had suffered an instantaneous cardiac arrest with no known trauma or cause. I was dead or certainly appeared to be on the way to being declared dead.

Literally, within seconds, two men, strangers to me, appeared on the scene and started to expertly apply CPR to start my heart, my human engine, again. They were my first miracle men. They were/are secret servicemen assigned to the UN. They happened to be there getting their brown bag lunches before returning to their stations. A police officer, Officer Riley, also appeared at the scene and immediately dialed 911. No later when he hung up from that call, an entire crew of emergency medical technicians (EMTs) from the NYC Fire Department were there with their vehicle pulled up onto the sidewalk on 44th Street and 1st Avenue. They had arrived before they were summoned by the 911 operator. Their official response time for my incident was ZERO minutes, ZERO seconds. That couldn't be luckier.

The EMTs saw the fuss and bother surrounding my prone body and moved quickly. The head of that crew was Mr. Byron Melo, a very experienced EMT and now a friend. They shocked my heart to revive it. Mr. Melo rapidly assessed the situation, gauged my condition, and chose to administer drugs immediately. Right on the street, he filled a hypodermic needle with a portion of special drugs designed to keep me alive and to prevent my brain from swelling (often the cause of death in cardiac arrest incidents). The EMTs also decided I needed immediate hospitalization as I showed no physical reaction to the shot. Officer Riley had Stewart Cahn retrieve my cell phone, and the officer called my home. Quite luckily, he reached Michelle, my wife, who, though a full-time real estate broker, just happened to be home for a few minutes. She had left some keys at home; the only reason she was there was to receive the officer's call and report that "I was down and en route to Bellevue Hospital." Michelle instinctively asked, "Is he dead?" "No," the officer said, making clear that I was unconscious and not being taken to Bellevue without good cause. The circumstances were life-threatening.

Our adult daughter Sharon was also available that day. She is a very competent driver. She drove Michelle directly into the city in just about record time. Michelle was there in time to give her consent to a procedure to put me into an induced coma. They needed my brain and body to repair themselves with the aid of the prescribed medications they would give me through intravenous applications while in a coma. They told her that I had to wake up in forty-eight to seventy-two hours if I were to wake at all. "What are his chances?" she asked. The doctors were very reluctant to speculate. Very reluctant.

Finally, Michelle cornered one young physician who would make a guesstimate. He said and threw open the possibility that I had a 5 to 15 percent chance to be revived as against 85 percent to 95 percent likelihood of an adverse result. Michelle had to speak to me (in my comatose state) before leaving the hospital. She told me that we had not completed our assigned work as a family. That was in 2012, and she said I had "more to do." Another officer, perhaps a security official of the hospital, watched Michelle's performance and later commented to her that she had done very well; she had gotten through to me. "Your husband feels your strength," he predicted.

Perhaps, the officer was right. I did survive. I am alive and well; it is eight years since then. I am eighty-one years old now, and I have finished other important works of a lifetime. My wife and I have traveled to many great places around the world, including to South Africa on a photographic safari. We have seen our three granddaughters *bat mitzvah*, and we have taken each of them on European tourist learning adventures. Michelle has enjoyed a fabulous career as likely the best residential real estate broker in our greater community, and I got to play the role of being her assistant's assistant while that happened, plus, I finally closed out profitably litigation that lasted almost eighteen years. We have helped Sharon relocate to South Florida. And, with the benefit of years of creative writing classes at LIU adult education, I have completed this presentation of a collection of Holocaust remembrances. I would not have been around to do that but for my survival on September 21, 2012, and those fortuitous circumstances.

The List

I saw the list, I saw the list
My family in Macedonia
My family, as Macedonians
Four hundred years before, gratefully
They responded to outstretched hands
Amazingly, the Ottoman Turks sent ships
Sent ships to rescue them, the unwanted
Escaping from a place they'd always called home.

Espanoles sin pais
Gingerly, carefully, they resettled
It wasn't easy, it wasn't always smooth
Neighbors in any neighborhood naturally
Would not appreciate the sudden infusion
Of 1000s of foreign speaking immigrants
It is tough to get along, communicate
See eye to eye on everything; It's tough

But, apparently, it happened
Generation after generation after generation
Somehow, they learned to live together
Perhaps, because the climate was right
Macedonia is in a temperate zone
Macedonians are a well-tempered people
Chiseled toughly, as the mountain faces
Roughly, kind and caring, is the case

My father had remembered
The flowers and the trees, beautifully
I learned abundant plants of many species
Pine forests with ferns and junipers
Oaks, sycamore, weeping willows, appropriately
Rich ecological life, befitting rich human lives
My father said: scenic mountains and pretty blue lakes
Banjas, and the kosher bakery right next door

Borders which shifted with the winds
An interesting, intriguing history
Byzantine, Slavs, Bulgars
Tsars, briefly even a Norman conquest
In the 20th century, Greeks, Turks, Bulgarians
My family enjoyed the fruits and vegetables
Spoeska salad, and the diversity
In Macedonia with the Macedonians

Spurred by the Balkans wars, ended 100 years before
Some Monastirli Macedonians became Americans
Pridefully, they transplanted a long ways away
They went about their new full lives, not forgetting
But not remembering, not remembering enough
Now, I saw the list, I saw the list from WWII
I did not know before, but now I know
My distant Macedonian cousins rode in those transports

My first reaction was shock and silent tears
How could it be, how did it happen, again
Another time, hateful, blameful, flames
I've read the names, our names
Cohen, Calderon, Aureste, many others
Familiar names, apparently they surrendered
Sad to imagine that they just gave up
But then, a saving grace, a minor footnote

Some of them had served as partisans as well
Against the fascist occupation, fought
Back to back with other Macedonians
Righteous, decent, indignant people
Seeking a free and independent Macedonia
Seeking, which they've now achieved
A free and independent Macedonia
Not sure why that matters, but it does to me
From this adult child of two families Monastirli
It matters that Macedonia is independent and free
Perhaps, because, it's possible and maybe even fair to say,
My distant cousins, your cousins, did not perish
Did not perish entirely, totally, in vain

don david Calderon y. Aroesty
April 28, 2013, revised August 10, 2017

March of 1943

Complicity with evil is evil
Resistance requires its own reward
Even then, there was mostly no earthly redemption

The March of murder began
With a signal event
In Koriukivka, the Ukraine
6,700 of the residents, all of them
Became victims of the German SS
The SS burned down the entirety of the City, all
Of its buildings, and then assassinated the survivors

In Berlin, on the 2nd of the month
1,500 Jewish men, women and children were
Captured in a roundup of what the Nazis called
Rats hiding from their rightful fate, allegedly
They were not harmed at all in Germany
They were "only" deported to Auschwitz
90 percent of them then were immediately executed upon arrival

On the 11th of the month, my entire extended family
The Sephardic Jews, Monastirli, of Macedonia
And all their cousins, and coreligionist friends
All of them, in Skopje, Stip and Bitola, all of them
Were collected for transport to Treblinka
The notorious German death camp, Treblinka
And, they too were gassed immediately upon arrival
More than 7,000 souls, good and true Sephardi Jews
Bulgarian soldiers had packaged the shipment

Finland signed a trade agreement with Germany
The Germans announced it, with beaming pride
They were providing food to the undernourished Finns
In what was described in the Axis press
As "traditional Finnish-German spirit of friendship"
In the same month, however, Finland was warned

By von Ribbentrop, German Foreign Minister
That the Nazis would not take lightly any Finnish
Attempt to leave the Axis or to make peace with the Allies
No wonder, von Ribbentrop warned Finland, in Denmark
Where the Germans permitted a free election, 3.3 percent
Practically nobody, nobody Danish, voted for the Nazis

Bulgaria, officially a German Nazi Axis power
Nonetheless, refused to comply with a German demand
That the Bulgarian Jews be deported to Nazi camps
Concentration camps, like Auschwitz and Treblinka
The Bulgarian Parliament revoked the deal to give up their Jews
As a result of the Bulgarian peoples' protests, and the efforts
Of the King, but no one protested what was happening
In Macedonia, with Bulgarian soldiers as the packagers
At the same time, the first of 19 transports of Greek Jews
46,000 persons in all, left Salonika in route to Auschwitz
By August 18th, that removal also would be completed

In Belarus, the entire population of a tiny village
The tiny village of Khatyan was attacked by SS soldiers
Germans from the 36th *Waffen Grenadier* Division
After four of their own, four Nazi officers, were killed
They, in turn, executed a plan of their version of just revenge
By burning down the entire village, the entire village
Killing 156 of the 160 residents of that tiny village

Gypsies, with typhus, were sent to the gas chambers
At Auschwitz, the first 1,700 of them to go, on the 22nd
Later, thousands more Gypsies, most surely without typhus,
Would meet the same fate, the Nazi death machines were
Working full-time, double time, overtime, murdering Jews
And many others, often forgotten in the telling, there were
Many, many others, including Priests and Catholic clergy
Who failed to fully abide by the Nazi rules and regulations

But, the news was not all bad, German submarines were losing battles
Battles they had previously won, and there were two unknown Germans
Who each attempted to assassinate Hitler; the tide of the war
Was changing, though changing too timidly, as Stalin saw it, in a letter
Written to Roosevelt in March of '43 requesting a western front immediately
Tho' D-Day would finally happen in '44, it was too late for millions of innocents
In March of 1943, Maria Restituta Kafka, an Austrian Roman Catholic nun,

Vigorously opposed to the Holocaust, did not make it to the gas chambers
She was beheaded in Austria, on orders of the murderer Martin Bormann

don david Calderon y. Aroesty
February 21, 2020

Pay attention to the winds and the words
They are a forewarning of the days to follow
Choosing the right path first assumes a choosing.

A Brush with History

On March 30, March 31, and April 1, 1992, my wife and I were in Spain. It was our fourth trip to Spain together; my fifth trip in total to Spain in the few years starting with 1984. The trips were made without a business reason. I had no business in Spain, no family in Spain, no known friends in Spain. These were personal trips, emotional trips. I had become entranced by an ancient historical connection I personally felt with Spain.

On those three days in 1992, we had the high honor and privilege of being in attendance at certain private and public events with King Juan Carlos and Queen Sophia, real monarchs, the royalty of the modern nation of Spain, a direct line to King Ferdinand and Queen Isabella, the original rulers in the fifteenth century. It was a "pinch me" moment for me and us. Here's how it happened.

****

My family, on both sides, lived in Spain prior to 1492. Jews are known to have lived in Spain for many centuries throughout the Common Era (CE). In the eighth century, the Moors (Moslems from North Africa) invaded Iberia and conquered Spain and Portugal. While no democratic ideals were achieved, and the Moors were gradually relegated to Grenada in the southern tip of Spain for much of the next five centuries, the Moors, the Catholics, and the Jews (possibly as much as 15 percent of the total population) were lived and worked together and achieved one of the most learned and advanced societies in the world; but the native Catholics felt oppressed by the control of their country by the Moors and as second class citizens within their own land.

Starting in about the 1200s, the Catholics commenced a war of *Reconquista* to throw the Moors out. The Jews of Spain largely tried to stay out of that struggle, but as the ally of neither, they soon became the volleyball in the middle, perceived as a possible prospective and enemy of both. It took almost three hundred years for the Spanish Catholics to prevail. In January of 1492, the remaining Moors fighting force surrendered and returned to North Africa. On March 31, 1492, King Ferdinand, the first king of a united Spain, issued a decree—the Edict of Expulsion—which required all the Jews of Spain to either convert or leave. The edict was published on April 30 of that year and gave the Jews three months until July 31, 1492, to get out or to declare themselves Christians. While the numbers are uncertain, roughly about half of the two hundred thousand Jews then living in Spain decided to convert, and the other half left. My forebears were among those who left.

The Ottoman Turks sent ships to the harbors of Spain to pick up the Spanish Jews and bring them back to Turkey and its territories, mostly in the Balkans. On July 31, 1492, folklore teaches me that my family members were in Turkish boats headed east in the Mediterranean to the Balkans, while at the very same time on August 3, 1492, Columbus's three ships left Spain heading first southwest to the Canary Islands and, from there, west via the Atlantic Ocean, trying to find a shortened water route to India. Columbus, of Italian Catholic heritage, was very religious and conscious of the other events happening at the time of his state-sponsored voyages of discovery, and his logs reflect that. Columbus is not considered a heroic figure in modern times; though his personal story and the voyages of discovery that uncovered the continents of America to the European world remain heroic to me.

My wife Michelle and I had been vacationing on a beach in Spain in 1984 before I had any concern with, or detailed understanding of, the foregoing history. Yes, of course, I knew that my parents were of "Spanish" or Sephardic origin. They spoke Spanish, actually a language called Ladino (a Judeo-Spanish dialect that dates back to fifteenth-century Castilian, with many idioms and significant pronunciation differences from Spanish). My maternal grandmother, who lived in Rochester, New York, in an insular Sephardic American community, spoke Ladino as her primary language.

On the beach in 1984, I read in a local newspaper of the Spanish government's intention to make many great events in 1992 to celebrate the quincentennial of the Columbus voyages of discovery of the new world and also specifically included their intention that 1992 be the year of the Sephardic Jew. *How wonderful*, I thought, and I clipped the newspaper article to bring it home. Once back in New York, I sent the article to a couple of Jewish organizations I knew. To my surprise, the initial reaction was less than positive. They showed little interest. Some people told me that the Spanish government was only doing that to detract attention from the negatives of the 1492 expulsion of the Jews. My own sense of history, though I am certainly not a historian, told me that there was more to be gained by shaking hands with the Spaniards in the twentieth century than by shaking our heads at them about events that had occurred five hundred years prior.

In 1988, the American Sephardi Federation, Mr. Leon Levy, decided to let me create a project, called Project Sepharad for us, as Sephardim, to respond affirmatively to the Spanish invitation. I started reading books about Sephardic history, Spanish history, the fifteenth century generally, and also about Columbus and the voyages of discovery. I attended certain events sponsored by the Spanish National Tourist Office, eventually becoming a speaker at those events.

As the first international organizing chairperson of Project Sepharad, one of the goals was to create a unified Jewish response and symbolic reunion with the Spanish people. In connection therewith, I envisioned, imagined, and wrote that the king of Spain ought to use the occasion to revoke the Edict of Expulsion. There were about fifteen thousand Jews peacefully and from all appearances happily living in Spain by 1992; there was surely no continuing expulsion. Any act of revocation would be only symbolic, and it was rightly considered impolitic for an outsider to rock the boat of coexistence for an act only of symbolism.

The government of Israel noted the events in Israel and encouraged Sephardim worldwide to respond affirmatively to Spain. In December of 1990, there was a conference in Jerusalem with representatives from many groups, including me, on behalf of the ASF and Project Sepharad. The Israeli message to the conferees was similar to what I had espoused: be positive and be organized.

Project Sepharad largely failed in its mission to have a united Jewish response to the Spanish invitation for 1992; but my efforts were adopted by Yeshiva University where Haham Rabbi Solomon Gaon, once the chief Sephardic rabbi in the United Kingdom, was a professor and a leading voice for Sephardic Jewry worldwide. Under Rabbi Gaon and his then very capable assistant, Rabbi Mitchell Serels, Yeshiva organized (and I participated in it) the Spanish National Tourist Office events and a very well-planned reunion trip to Zaragoza, Spain, in 1991. In Zaragoza, we held well-attended Jewish services for the first time in five hundred years. We also had a weeks' worth of visits to small towns in the northeastern quadrant of Spain where I learned a lot more from the locals about the connections between the Spaniards and the Sephardim and the families of the Nuevo Catolicas who had converted in 1492 and remained in Spain. I also had a separate trip to Toledo where a small museum was being established to display a little information about Sephardic history for the anticipated visitors in 1992. The then mayor of Toledo told me that "the Jewish roots of Spain" was then the most popular adult education course at the local college.

Later, I learned with great pride and pleasure that the king—on his own initiative or responding to requests from a small Spanish Jewish contingent—had decided to revoke the Edict of Expulsion on March

31, 1992. Michelle and I were honored to receive an invitation to attend the revocation event at the main synagogue in Madrid. Our brush with history commenced that weekend with a tour of one of Madrid's famous museums on Friday, the thirtieth, a tour led by Queen Sophia. On the following day, the streets of Madrid were full of Spanish and Israeli flags, dancing together in the wind, hanging from thousands of the city's streetlamps. In the synagogue on Saturday, King Juan Carlos, there together with the president of Israel, gave a marvelous and, to me, unforgettable speech—front-page news in the *New York Times* and elsewhere worldwide. In brief, his theme was "who lost" by the expulsion of the Jews, and his answer was "we" (all of Spain of every denomination) had lost by the forced separation and by surrendering some of its most valuable citizens.

On the third day, we were part of about a fifty-person contingent invited into the castle to spend a brief period of time with the king and queen. It was on the thirtieth; however, I felt most especially blessed when the king of Spain gave the Prince of Asturias prize, effectively Spain's Nobel prize that came with a $50,000 stipend, to Haham Rabbi Gaon for his friendship and leadership of the Sephardim in their renewed connection to Spain. I had been personally present externally to their room when the two of them met privately and engaged in a brief discussion. Reading a news article on a beach in 1984 and following up on it had led me to an amazing place and an extraordinary brush with historical experience. "Afitar" is not a word that can be found in a Spanish dictionary, though, surely, Spanish/Castilian in origin, and in *Ladino,* it means "coincidence" with a connotation of being mystical.

I do not need a DNA test to know I am partly Spanish; I feel "Spanish." When surveys ask about my ethnic origin, I often check the box that says Hispanic. I am not fluent in the Spanish language, though I should be. While traveling in Spain on those various trips, I remember being able to comprehend well, even if tongue-tied to speak the right words myself.

I have also become proud of my family's four hundred plus years in Turkish Macedonia. I feel indebted to Moslem Turkey for opening its doors to the Spanish Jews in 1492 and also have great respect and kinship for the Macedonian people.

In the Ottoman Empire, the Sephardim retained their Spanish language and many of the customs of their former homeland. We spoke *Ladino*, our Spanish-based language (indeed some of our words became part of the Macedonian lexicon, [e.g., banja (bath) to mean spa]); ate Spanish foods; sang and danced to Spanish tunes; and reminisced about the former homeland from which we had been evicted. Our prayers and hymns, primarily in Hebrew, continued and continued to this day to be partially in *Ladino*.

The remembrances in this book include some that specifically relate to the *Sephardim* and the events relating to the Nazi assaults upon them. In one remembrance, specifically "Tolerance and Intolerance," I connected the special efforts of four Claretian priests to help Sephardic Jews escape from Nazi-controlled France in the 1940s to Spain to the 1992 revocation of the Edict of Expulsion.

OTHER OBSERVATIONS

Cemetery Stones

We've seen this scene before
It is ugly and disturbing
1,000 cemetery stones overturned
Some broken or splintered, all wounded
Inexplicably; there was nothing to be gained
By the vandals, nothing lost by the deceased
But the impact on the living is both overwhelmingly
Sad, and sickeningly frightening, that "they" hate us
Whoever they are, they hate us so much, so very much
That even death is not a barrier to them

No one would rationally risk
The commission of penal crimes, punishable
By fines and imprisonment, only just
Just to make a meaningless statement
They, the living ghosts who raid the cemeteries
They're intending by their random violence to communicate
It is difficult to imagine, almost impossible
To explain, we are at once atop the mountain
Proud and secure, we thought, we knew
And insecure, afraid, because we thought we knew

And, that is their message
We do not know, we cannot even conceive
That there may be inland oceanic
Waves, higher than the sky
Foreclosing all of the sunlight, all reason and rationality
Blaspheming the dead is not, not their only intention
They seek to make the living shudder and wonder
About the coming days without sunlight, and with long nights
If we pass, when we pass away, where will our graves be?
When will our lives ever be free? Free from such disturbances
Threatened prospects of indecency lasting beyond memory

March 10, 2017

Wyatt Earp's ashes are buried in a Jewish cemetery
American frontiersman, gambler, vagabond
Famous for winning the gunfight at the OK Corral
Involved in many tiffs with many toughs
And though he also served as deputy sheriff/marshal
His reputation was surely sorely tarnished in many incidents
His complex soul is standing guard perpetually at Eternity Hills
There are lessons in Earp's troubled life and eventless death
We must live and love tumultuously and win the fights at hand
There is no sense worrying about living ghosts hiding in darkness.

God Is Interdenominational
(Madeline's Bat Mitzvah Lesson)

God is good
God is great
It is a basic tenet
Of our faith
That there is but one God

But, God has many names
In many different nations
For many different people
Of many, many different faiths

So, if our God is going to be
As good as God could possibly be
And, as great as any one God might ever be
It stands to reason then, be purely rational, that
God must most assuredly be interdenominational.

don david Calderon y. Aroesty
October 22, 2016

**We do not uniquely own a good and great God
It is more genuinely faithful and appropriate
To fully understand and entirely appreciate
That God owns us, among many different people
Omnisciently, God oversees many different faiths.**

A Would-Be Suicide Bomber
An Advocate for Peace

She knew
She knew that once she put on the belt
There would be no turning back
No possibility of revocation, return
To a life of uneventful ordinary events

She knew the explosives would
Rip her apart, from limb to limb
Reducing her to a bloody pulp
Leaving no part of her body un-injured
Leaving her daughter, as an orphan

She had good cause, she thought
To do this radical act, good cause indeed
She had lived, day to day, week to week
Month to month, now year to year
With anger, despair, hopelessness

She had enough of it, standing still was no solution
"They come to take our land, maybe that we could
Understand, but they take our souls too
We become as if nonpersons, lacking integrity
Denied the ability to stand up for ourselves"

Monkeys in the organ pipers carousel
They are the scientists and the entrepreneurs
We are, the fortunate of us, the hairdressers
And the taxi drivers, the shleppers,
The schlubs and the schlemiels

Her former husband, a distant cousin,
Had been a classic schlemiel
He could never make a living
He could hardly even try, or so it seemed

Before he ran away, and disappeared
From his wife, her life

Revolution is necessary and yet impossible
They have all the tanks and helicopters
We have only empty fantasies of revenge
The fantasies are unhelpful, they eat at our core
Creating illusions of spectacular successes
and deep feelings of regret

We wish the world was shaped differently
We wish the Nazis had never existed; they caused this conflict
Or, perhaps, if only, the Jews had fought back then,
Instead of running away, landing on our land
My jihad is to send a message, God truly decides

God decides between right and wrong, who lives and dies
They are conquerors and we are conquered; God decides
All we seek is peace and balance, a flat earth approach
Not one with tops and bottoms, masters and serfs
Nowhere is it written, nowhere is it required
that we shall kneel to them

Shifa al-Qudsi's plan to be a suicide bomber was interrupted
She was arrested, convicted and imprisoned
In jail, she had time to reconsider, replan, reorganize
God decides, she concluded again, and God needs
No more suicide bombers, to help the parties find a new balance

She became an active combatant for peace
"Disturbing the peace in an unpeaceful place
Can never be a crime, any more than robbing
A bank which does not handle any money"
The proper goal is to stop all bloodshed on both sides

She became a combatant for a progressive peace
She read, she learned, she respected Gandhi, Mandela, Dr. King
"I am not afraid," she said, to violent critics on both sides
"I have seen the mountain and the mountain has seen me"
"I have climbed the mountain, and together, together we shall be free."

November 3, 2016

Rejoinder to a Would-Be Suicide Bomber

Loving Israel does not close my eyes
My ears, my mind or my heart
To the anguished cries of others
To the plight of those Palestinians

We have nearly six thousand years
Of experience, experiencing the travails
Of combatants for a progressive peace
We are, we are the original Palestinians
Punished and penalized for being such
Anti-Semitism applies to all Semites

We too have seen the mountains and the valleys
We know what it is to feel hopelessness and despair
Together, if there can be a road to togetherness
Together, we can, we must, find a way to repair
To rebuild God's paradise, in the place
Where it was originally, in the place we both call home.

November 4, 2016

Charlottesville

The scariest part of it
They came from the past to be a part of the present
They came from the dark to be in plain sight
They had no reason, were given no reason
To hide their identifications, they were there for a fight
They announced their intentions, planned and marched right in

They brought weapons and insignia, signs proclaiming
They were intending to Make America Great Again
That's what the new President promised, they would make it true
To make America great again, they had to deal with the "knee-grows" and the Jews
Both of whom, they asserted, had become too big for their britches
"Those sons of bitches, trampling on our history and our land"

This is their contentions: In World War Two, we were on the wrong side, you see
We should have been allied with the Germans and the Nazis
It's O.K., perfectly O.K., for them to wave the swastikas
Do straight arm salutes and signal *seig heil*, because
The Germans and the Nazis, for all their faults, made this a better place
Made this a better place, by cleansing Europe of the inferior race and races

In the United States of America, especially the good ole Confederate States
In their view, the world's been turned upside down completely inexplicably
For the last eight years, they've suffered a foreign born African President
With a suspicious phony birth certificate, our current President rightly doubted
But he'd been shouted down, by the Jew news media, totally FAKE, fake news
It's time, they claim, for their new crew to torchlight the beginning of another coup

More, they propound, there was nothing wrong with segregation, it was Constitutional
Until the Court was stacked with Jews, Jews and Catholics deciding all
Practically no chance for a regular straight Christian white man to be standing tall
The LGBT femmes have taken over; it feels like it's been almost a millennium
Since California had any Senator at all with both a backbone and a click, the others are
Turning our public schools into multicolored cesspools with genderless bathroom tricks

Our borders have been intentionally left grossly negligently unprotected
Allowing all those sunbrowned criminals and rapists to invade, steal our jobs, and vote
Millions of them illegally voted in the last election, all voting for more corruption

There's a Congressional investigation to prove it, but the Latinistas won't permit it
The bad news boys in Jew York and Washington, DC, are gayly daily covering up
Others still making believe Hillary won, seeking to deny us even moral victory
Our best chance ever to reshape America entirely, to Make America White Again

That's what they were marching for, the neo-Nazis, KKK and white supremacists
To show that it was them, them who won the election, they claim the difference
That they made the difference, they'd have us believe, in Florida, and South Carolina
In Michigan and Wisconsin too, in many, many other States, the mighty right rose again
And, it wasn't only in Dixie, sure enough, it was in the whole righteous nation, they
Assert, all participated in the revolution, they engendered, encouraged and made true

****

Charlottesville was claimed to be a dispute about the removal of a statue
A statue honoring Robert E. Lee, a confederate general and master military tactician
There's a whole lot of Americans, not all of whom are Black, who don't want there to be
Statues honoring slave owners, slavery defenders and fighters against American ideals
And, there's a whole lot of Americans, not all of whom are liberals, who admire
Abraham Lincoln's Gettysburg address, and Nelson Mandela's philosophy,
In favor of simply letting history be history as a means to going forward hopefully

It ought to be plain to see, the battle at Charlottesville was not about General Lee
That was only the subtext, an excuse for the vicious to be vicious publicly
A large group of counterprotesters, idealists, hoped to expose the march of hate as hate
The President, we have only one President at a time, said there were many fine people
Fine people, on both sides of the line, and bad people among the counterprotesters
While he at least twice condemned the neo-Nazis and the KKK,
The references to fine people resonated with friend and foe alike

The most important question of the day, still lingering and unresolved
Did he say even once, did he tell them, you've got the wrong idea, making America
Great Again was not intended, is not intended, will never be intended,
To spike hatred against Blacks, coloreds and Jews. or any class or sect
If only he had said that, if only he had said, what we've achieved so far together
Was made possible also by the building blocks during the Presidency of Barack Obama

And graciously embraced his predecessor as a former President, to signal appropriately,
One America, Black and white, European and Asian, children of immigrants all
If only he'd addressed the David Dukes of the collective hate brigade, telling them
"I do not want your support, I disown any notion that Making America Great Again
Is an opening for hate I intend to be, will be, the President, of and for all Americans;
That includes my Jewish grandchildren." If, only if, the President could be a **mensch**.

The most important question of the day, still lingering and unresolved
Is this Administration wrongly intending to spike hatred between us
Or rightly committed, Constitutionally, to one America, Black and White
We are, and will always be, a nation of immigrants and many fresh faces
An amalgamation, blend and combination, made stronger by our alliance
Our alliance with one another, for one United States of America.
Hate may march, some may pardon it; love, respect and decency will prevail

don david Calderon y. Aroesty
August 26, 2017

Second Appendix

Prepared by Gabrielle Flamm
West Chester University of Pennsylvania
Holocaust and Genocide Studies
November 15, 2018
For the Remembrances Project

Recommended for Teenagers and Young Adults

- The Diary of a Young Girl—Anne Frank
- Prisoner B-3987—Alan Gratz
- Nightingale—Kristin Hannah
- The Librarian of Auschwitz—Antonio Iturbe
- Number the Stars—Lois Lowry
- Sarah's Key—Tatiana de Rosnay
- Yellow Star—Jennifer Roy
- Maus—Art Spiegelman
- Milkweed—Jerry Spinelli
- Edith's Story—Edith Velmans
- The Devil's Arithmetic—Jan Yolen
- The Book Thief—Markus Zusak

Recommended for Young Adults

- I Have Lived a Thousand Years—Livia Bitton Jackson
- Schindler's List—Thomas Keneally
- Survival in Auschwitz—Primo Levi
- If I Should Die Before I Wake—Han Yolen
- Auschwitz—Laurence Rees
- The Pianist—Wladyslaw Szpilman
- The Night—Elie Wiesel

Historical Research

- A History of the Holocaust—Yeuda Bauer
- Ordinary Men—Christopher Browning
- Origins of the Nazi Genocide—Henry Friedlander
- The Nazi Dictatorship—Ian Kershaw
- History on Trial—Deborah Lipstadt
- Emergence of Jewish Ghettos in Nazi-Occupied Europe—Dan Michman

Holocaust Museums
and Memorials

Wikipedia maintains a list of Holocaust museums and memorials in the United States. The list is twelve pages long and includes seventy-five sites in thirty-one different states from Maine to Arizona and California. The most important and most resource-filled site is the United States Memorial Museum in Washington, DC. Other important locations include the Museum of Jewish History in Manhattan, New York, down near Battery Park. The survivors of the Shoah Visual History Foundation at the University of Southern California (Los Angeles), Illinois Holocaust Museum and Education Center (Skokie), and University of Michigan Holocaust Memorial, Raoul Wallenberg Place (Ann Arbor). The more important point is that for most Americans within the continental US, a Holocaust memorial or museum is easily reached, and if not, there is a public library with a large number of books and other publications about the subject.

Graphic Illustrations
Included in Remembrances

Name of illustration	Referencing prose poems
Butterflies	Vol 1, 7; Vol. 1, 8
White Lion	Vol 1, 4
White Roses	Vol 1, 12
Headless Nazi Operating Guillotine	Vol 1, 12; March of 1943. App.
Award Winner	Vol 1, 14
Guiding Principles in the Carpathian Mountains	Vol 1, 16
Greatest Gymnast Ever	Vol 2, 9
Over the Rainbow	Vol 1, 11
Garden of Jars	Vol 2, 17
Heart of Gold	Vol. 1, 9
Monster in the Bottle	Vol 3, 19; Vol 3, 7
The Train Station	Vol 3, 1
Anne Frank's Chestnut Tree	Vol 1, 2
Beneath a Scarlet Sky	Vol 3, 8

About the Author

D, David Cohen is a retired business, corporate and securities lawyer who lives in Roslyn. (Long Island), New York. He is of Sephardic Jewish ancestry. His family lived in Spain prior to 1492, and in the Ottoman Empire (Macedonia, specifically) until 1913. when his father, then a child, emigrated to the United States. David has always been aware of and involved with his Sephardic, Spanish speaking (*Ladino)* heritage. His search for more information and understanding about the Holocaust began with him reading the list of the Jewish residents of Macedonia who were transported to and killed at Treblinka in 1943. He has written this book in his Sephardic nom-de-plume, don david Calderon y. Aroesty. In his business life, David graduated from Duke University Law School (1965), and also attained a Masters in Business from Columbia University (1977). He has been a New York lawyer mostly representing publicly-owned companies in transactions and matters throughout the United States, Puerto Rico and certain places in Europe. He and his wife, Michelle, have traveled widely internationally. David is also a survivor of cardiac arrest (9/21/2012) which he connects to his desires to present the "Remembrances and Other Observations."

CPSIA information can be obtained
at www.ICGtesting.com
Printed in the USA
BVHW020522151022
649324BV00002BA/9